In a day when the merit of the many, including many Ch biblically grounded presentati affirms the gospel for the Jew... ... keep his promises to Israel. How do these go together? This book takes us well down the path to a theologically sound answer.

Darrell L. Bock, Ph.D.
Research Professor of New Testament Studies
Professor of Spiritual Development and Culture
Dallas Theological Seminary
Former President of the Evangelical Theological Society

The contributors to this book exhibit the kind of scholarly balance necessary for moving the debate concerning modern Israel from the practice of firing shots from opposing trenches to a careful examination of the facts in the light of Biblical Revelation. As to the importance of their contributions, the declared ideological motivations of groups like Hamas, who vow to put an end to Israel as a sovereign state, mean that the question of modern Israel's existence must be approached in essentially theological terms.

Ronald E. Diprose, Ph.D.
Academic Dean, Istituto Biblico Evangelico Italiano, Rome
Author of Israel and the Church: The Origin and Effects of Replacement Theology *(Waynesboro, GA, Authentic Media, 2004).*

A book of this quality, character and courage has been needed for decades! I want to congratulate Dr. Calvin Smith of King's Evangelical Divinity School for engaging in this highly charged and controversial study focusing on God's plan for the Jewish people, the nation of Israel and the Arab world. I further applaud the project for taking the very critical next step of helping to provide a matrix for understanding the relationship between the Western Church and the Christian, Messianic and Muslim communities of the East.

Mitch Glaser, Ph.D.
President, Chosen People Ministries

There is a belated tide rising against almost virulent anti-Judaism. So in *The Jews, Modern Israel and the New Supercessionism* Dr. Calvin Smith provides us with a rich resource that covers the essential issues at a substantial level. The times call for a volume like this. May it help turn Christians toward a more Judeo-centric eschatology. Supremely may it uphold the glory of the quintessential Jew, the Lord Jesus Christ, who shall return as a Jew.

Dr Barry E. Horner
Author of Future Israel: Why Christian Anti-Judaism Must Be Challenged. *New American Commentary Studies in Bible and Theology (Nashville, TN: Broadman and Holman, 2007).*

A large portion of the word of God in the Old Testament is being misinterpreted or deliberately avoided by those who have adopted the teaching that the Christian Church has replaced Israel and that the ancient promises made by God to Abraham, Isaac, Jacob and David are now *passé.* However, Calvin L. Smith has edited a set of chapters in a new book that makes a vital contribution towards rectifying this imbalance in interpretation. May it spark a long-overdue discussion among Evangelical interpreters of all persuasions as well as one between Jewish people of the book and believers in the Christian Church.

Walter C. Kaiser, Jr., Ph.D.
Colman Mockler Distinguished Emeritus Professor of Old Testament, President Emeritus, Gordon Conwell Theological Seminary

At last, everything you needed to know about replacement theology. With seven distinct voices, each covering one aspect of this aberration, we now have a definitive text book that ought to be in the library of every serious Christian place of learning.

Steve Maltz
British Christian broadcaster and popular author of The Land of Many Names, The People of Many Names, *and* Jesus, Man of Many Names.

Any scholarly attempt to address the growth of supercessionism should be welcomed in the Evangelical community worldwide. While not perfect, modern Israel is thought by most Evangelicals to be a fulfilment of biblical prophecy, and therefore to be seen as one of the formidable signs of Christ's soon return. Dr. Calvin Smith has taken on this challenge, and brought us a strong rebuttal to the position held by supercessionists, and must be thanked for giving Evangelical Christians this important compilation of writings by such a group of authors. Thanks.

Rev. Dr. Daniel Mercaldo
Senior Pastor and Founder
Church at the Gateway, Staten Island, New York

Considered and nuanced discussion of God's purpose for Israel is sometimes in short supply. This book plays an important role providing just such a discussion.

Mark S. Sweetnam, Ph.D.
Research Fellow at Trinity College, Dublin

The Jews, Modern Israel and the New Supercessionism provides thorough insights, both biblical and secular, into issues related to the present, past, and future status of ethnic Israel. It is heartening that editor Calvin L. Smith along with an assortment of contributors has outlined many historic and current facets related to present-day Israel. The availability and helpfulness of the book will strike a strong note in response to growing supercessionist influences regarding God's promises to Abraham and his descendants.

Dr Robert L. Thomas
Professor of New Testament Language and Literature
The Master's Seminary, Sun Valley, California

The articles in this book, written by scholars who vary in their theological stance, are balanced and profound. They seek to answer biblically some of the oldest heresies in the Church, which sadly are advocated by many Evangelicals today, namely that all the promises to Israel have been transferred to the Church and that Israel has ceased to be within God's purpose for world redemption. I warmly commend this book and pray that it will be widely read.

David W. Torrance
Retired Church of Scotland minister and author (with Howard Taylor) of Israel, God's Servant: God's Key to the Redemption of the World *(Milton Keynes: Paternoster, 2007).*

Finally, an irenic but yet resolutely Evangelical treatment of the issues surrounding the Middle Eastern crises centered around the contemporary state of Israel! While readers will agree or not depending on their own ideological biases, all who approach this book with an open mind will come away better informed about why Bible-believing Evangelicals think the Jews remain God's people in a distinctive way and why we can be hopeful that the good news of the gospel is still applicable in the present situation for all parties involved – Israelis and Palestinians, Jews and Arabs, and Christians of every ethnicity bound up on the conflict. As valuable is the attempt of the essayists to find a middle way between the extremes of Zionism on the one side and anti-Israelism on the other. The result is registration of an important set of mediating Evangelical voices in an otherwise tumultuous discussion.

Amos Yong, PhD.
Professor of Systematic Theology
Director of the Doctor of Philosophy Program
School of Divinity, Regent University, Virginia

The Jews, Modern Israel and the New Supercessionism

Resources for Christians

The Jews, Modern Israel and the New Supercessionism

Resources for Christians

edited by

Calvin L. Smith

King's Divinity Press
Lampeter, United Kingdom

Contents

About the Contributors   vii

Foreword by Mitch Glaser   ix

Preface by Mark S. Sweetnam   xiii

Acknowledgements   xv

Introduction   1

1   Who is the "Israel" of Romans 11:26?   8
     Andy Cheung

2   Biblical Theology and the Modern State of Israel   25
     Calvin L. Smith

3   Apostolic Jewish-Christian Hermeneutics   47
     and Supercessionism
     Jacob Prasch

4   A Calvinist Considers Israel's Right to the Land   63
     Stephen M. Vantassel

5   Israel and the Purposes of God   83
     Howard Taylor

6   Jealous for Zion: Evangelicals, Zionism and the   97
     Restoration of Israel
     Paul Richard Wilkinson

7 Faith and Politics in the Holy Land Today   119
   Calvin L. Smith

8 Is the Gospel Relevant to the Jewish People?   139
   Tony Pearce

Scripture Index   159

About the Contributors

Andy Cheung holds degrees with the Universities of Durham and Bangor and is currently completing a Ph.D. in linguistics and Bible translation at the University of Birmingham. He lectures in biblical languages and New Testament at King's Evangelical Divinity School.

Tony Pearce leads the Bridge Lane Christian Fellowship in Golders Green, London. He speaks widely, broadcasts regularly and has written several popular books on issues relating to Jewish evangelism and Christian responses to modern Israel.

Jacob Prasch is the founder of Moriel Ministries and teaches widely on Jewish-Christian hermeneutics. A fluent Hebrew speaker, he is a visiting lecturer at King's Evangelical Divinity School where he teaches Jewish-Christian Studies.

Calvin L. Smith (Ph.D., University of Birmingham) is Principal of King's Evangelical Divinity School and edits the *Evangelical Review of Society and Politics*. He is also a tutor for several British universities. He speaks widely on Israel and is currently writing a book exploring Christianity in the Holy Land for publication with Paternoster in 2010.

Howard Taylor has served as a missionary, minister and university lecturer, as well as teaching and lecturing widely in ethics, science and religion. He co-authored *Israel God's Servant: God's Key to the Redemption of the World* (Paternoster, 2007) with David W. Torrance.

Stephen M. Vantassel (Ph.D., Trinity Seminary, Indiana) lectures in biblical studies and systematic theology at King's Evangelical Divinity School and is Adjunct Professor at Trinity Seminary, Indiana. He also co-edits the *Evangelical Review of Society and Politics*.

Paul Richard Wilkinson (Ph.D., University of Manchester, England) is the author of *For Zion's Sake: Christian Zionism and the Role of John Nelson Darby* (Paternoster 2007). He is currently writing in the areas of dispensationalism, philo-Semitism and the Holocaust.

Foreword

You are about to embark on a theological journey to the Holy Land. The path will take you through the valleys of Scripture and the mountains of theological debate to the contemporary socio-political plains of the Middle East. Along the way, you will be introduced (or perhaps re-introduced) to a band of articulate, intelligent and biblically astute authors who will serve as your guides.

As a Messianic Jew for almost forty years, I can tell you that a book of this quality, character and courage has been needed for decades! I want to congratulate Dr. Calvin Smith of King's Evangelical Divinity School for engaging in this highly charged and controversial study focusing on God's plan for the Jewish people, the nation of Israel and the Arab world. I further applaud the project for taking the very critical next step of helping to provide a matrix for understanding the relationship between the Western Church and the Christian, Messianic and Muslim communities of the East.

It would be a sad mistake to underestimate the theological, political and even ecclesiastical challenge that Christians – both Jewish and Gentile – face in engaging the Muslim world for Christ. This book makes a profound contribution and provides information that is both biblical and relevant, thereby enabling followers of Jesus the Messiah to pray intelligently and thoughtfully consider our personal perspectives on issues relating to Israel and the Arab world. I view exploring our biblical roots and the complex, contemporary realities of the Middle East as a pilgrimage.

We cannot treat Israel as simply one nation among others. We also cannot view the Jewish people as just one people among many ethnic or religious groups, because we love the Jewish Messiah and we believe the Bible's story, which primarily takes place in Israel. Christians throughout the centuries have always recognized, rightfully, that there is something special about the land of Israel and the Jewish people. You will appreciate the chapter by Howard Taylor, who makes reference to the following quote by Mark Twain regarding the special role of Israel and the Jewish people:

> *The Egyptian, the Babylon and the Persian rose, filled the planet with sound and splendor, then faded to dream stuff and passed away; the Greek and the Roman followed, and made a vast noise, and they are gone; other peoples have sprung up and held their torch high for a time, but it burned out, and they sit in twilight now, or have vanished. The Jews saw them all, beat them all, and is now what he always was exhibiting no decadence, no infirmities of age, no weakening of his parts, no slowing of his energies, no dulling of his alert and aggressive mind. All things are mortal but the Jews; all other forces pass but he remains. What is the secret of his immortality?* (page 72)

A Substantial Contribution

Whatever your current perspective on Israel, the Jewish people, and the Middle East conflict, it is safe to say that these topics are especially unavoidable for thoughtful, growing believers in Jesus.

It is possible that you may never board a plane destined for the Holy Land (although it is an experience not to be missed!). You may never walk where Jesus walked and experience the land of the Bible first-hand, but through this book you can journey to the homeland of our Savior and gain a greater understanding of His "kinsmen according to the flesh." Eminent, capable, and well-informed scholars who have thought deeply about these subjects will guide you along the way.

I am grateful to Dr. Smith for the privilege of encouraging you, dear reader, to do more than simply skim this multi-author volume, but rather to read this book with a marker and an open Bible. You will want to study these chapters and talk over the issues raised with fellow believers and your pastor, as I am certain you will find the issues in this book to be critical to your faith.

I want to further commend the editor and authors for their evident passion for their subjects. They write with both mind and heart. They also strive to be fair and just in their portrayals of Jews and Arabs, Christians, Messianic Jews and Muslims. Each writer wrestles with the scriptural data as well as the books, articles and public relations information generated on these subjects.

A Balanced Approach
There's no doubt that an intelligent, biblically-based, politically astute and fair-minded volume is necessary to help Christians rebalance their views on the Middle East. I appreciate the authors' attempts to present both sides of the issues as much as possible. It is clear that this volume is attempting to rebalance the way in which Christians view the conflict in the Middle East. For many years, some evangelical Christians have been pro-Israel to the point of losing objectivity – and this certainly needs to be rebalanced. Some Christians have been driven by their eschatology to make claims and projections that have been embarrassing to many believers. As an American, I can tell you that this has been true on both sides of the pond and is not simply a concern of Christians in the United Kingdom.

But in the United Kingdom and North America as well as in Western Europe, there has been a recent pro-Palestinian swing that has pushed the church to a new stage of imbalance, as the title of the book suggests by coining the term "New Supercessionism." We cannot seek the welfare of Palestinians at the expense of Israel and the Jewish people. Unfortunately, this has been the case recently, as evidenced by the plethora of Christian books "bashing" Israel and the Jewish people.

While reading many of the books recently published about the Middle East, one gets the impression that Palestinians can do no wrong and that all the problems in the Middle East are a result of Israeli aggression. This book seeks to rebalance this perception and clarify the ways in which Islamic fundamentalists are a threat to the church, the West, and especially to Arab Christians. A number of the authors will suggest that in certain Christian circles, we have merely sanctified fundamentalist Islamic propaganda.

I have also had a deep and growing concern about the way in which the role of Jewish people in the Bible has been linked to the modern state of Israel. Of course this is true to a degree, but it is also problematic. The many popular Christian books that have promoted a pro-Palestinian Christian platform have led many in the church to lose their concern for Jewish evangelism. Great Britain has more than 400,000 Jewish people, and each one who has not already received Jesus as Saviour needs the Gospel.

I had a conversation with a Christian pro-Palestinian spokesman who has written a number of influential books that I believe have led to the imbalance that this current book attempts to correct. I asked him whether he realized that his books were actually helping to swing the Church beyond a pro-Palestinian position to one rapidly becoming anti-Israel and even anti-Jewish. I knew this was not his intention, yet it was the regrettable result of an overzealous Christian pro-Palestinian position.

Some Christians today feel that we cannot speak favourably about the need for Jewish evangelism without adding that reaching Arabs is important too! It is as if promoting Jewish evangelism is deemed unfair to Arabs, and that reaching Jewish people in London or New York City is tantamount to supporting all of Israel's political policies. There is a confusion between modern Israel and the Jewish people in general, which is hurting Jewish missions on both sides of the pond as Christians trend towards a more pro-Palestinian and anti-Israel position.

The ecclesiastical atmosphere has been profoundly charged against Israel and the Jewish people, and while many of us involved in Messianic ministry were wondering how to rebalance the viewpoint of the church, Dr. Smith and his team had already held a conference and now produced this essential volume of essays.

We now have a book that is biblical, fair, and honest, and will hopefully enrich Christians who love the Jewish people as well as the Palestinian people and who desire to see both Jews and Muslims come to Christ. This book provides the insights and theological framework for that critical and necessary balance.

Read each chapter carefully and enjoy the journey!

Mitch Glaser, Ph.D.
President, Chosen People Ministries
New York (31 March 2009)

Preface

"The gifts and calling of God are," Paul reminds us in Romans 11:29, "without repentance." Standing on their own, these words constitute a great statement about the character and attributes of God, a statement that must be of enormous value to every Christian. These words confirm to us that our God is neither fickle nor faithless, and that our relationship with Him has a deep and enduring permanence. In the context, of course, these words have a particular application to Israel. In the great unfolding of God's redemptive purpose which occupies the Apostle under the inspiration of the Holy Spirit, in this glorious epistle, God's continuing interest in His ancient people provides a telling index of the greatness of His faithfulness. And, for the believer in the Lord Jesus Christ today, the faithfulness of God to Israel is a source of wonder and reassurance, and an invaluable insight into the character of the God that we have come to know. Therefore, while it is true that a denial of God's future purpose for Israel robs that nation of its special place, that is only a beginning: it also impoverishes the Church and, most seriously of all, touches the glory and greatness of God.

This book collects contributions from a diverse collection of people who approach their subject from a diversity of doctrinal and disciplinary perspectives. They are united in this diversity by a common belief that God has not finished with Israel, that His irrevocable promises and commitment to the nation have not been made over wholesale to the church. In the text of Scripture and in the texture of history, the contributors to this important and valuable collection find affirmation upon affirmation of the centrality of Israel to God's great redemptive programme.

In their understanding of Scripture, the essays in this volume eschew any suggestion that Israel has been either replaced or superseded by the church. In an oftentimes complex ethical and political context that has revitalised approaches that continue the long and inglorious history of replacement theology, it is an important contribution to restate firmly, clearly and without polemical excess the conviction that such theologies are void of scriptural warrant and misrepresent our God. For the apostles, the challenges of evangelising

xiii

a pagan and oftentimes hostile gentile world never required the marginalisation of God's commitment to Israel. It would be difficult to concede that the challenges of our own time, formidable though they undoubtedly are, require any such reinterpretation on our part.

The authors of these essays have avoided polemical indiscretion in addressing the claims of replacement theology. But they have also been careful to be moderate in their approach to Israel. This is important for, as much as we may deplore the very idea of a replacement theology, we do well to avoid the excesses of a militant Zionism that often seems to extend its identification with Israel to the point of exemplifying the zeal not according to knowledge of which Paul speaks in Romans 10:2. To go beyond the warrant of Scripture in belligerent – even bellicose – support for the State of Israel, and to endorse all the actions of the State, is not to glorify God. It is also to ignore one of the plainest themes of Old Testament Scripture. The record of God's dealings with His people makes it very clear that His sovereign choice of Israel imparted, as well as immense privilege, enormous responsibility. Biblical Israel learned repeatedly that God demands a high standard of those with whom He associates His name, and we need to profit from their lessons. God's continued interest in Israel emphasises His righteousness and we cannot condone or endorse behaviour – whether national or individual – that runs counter to that standard.

At the end of Romans 11, Paul, having surveyed the greatness and grandeur of God's redemptive programme responds in the only appropriate way: 'O the depth of the riches both of the wisdom and knowledge of God! how unsearchable are His judgments, and His ways past finding out!' (Romans 11:33 KJV). Worship, then, is Paul's response to the riches of Divine grace as expressed in the gospel. The essays in this volume such exercise the mind. They should touch our hearts. But they will have their greatest success if, in reminding us of God's unwavering love for His ancient people, they prompt our spirits to worship the One who in matchless grace has revealed Himself as the God of Abraham, of Isaac, and of Jacob.

Mark Sweetnam, Ph.D.
Research Fellow, Trinity College, Dublin
Dublin (23 March 2009)

xiv

Acknowledgements

This book represents the work of various people to whom I am deeply indebted. Foremost among these, of course, are the contributors themselves, who not only prepared written papers for this volume but also delivered them at the conference on supercessionism out of which this book has arisen. I am exceedingly grateful, too, to Mitch Glaser and Mark Sweetnam for kindly providing a foreword and preface respectively. Both their confidence in the work and gracious words are greatly appreciated and indeed deeply encouraging, as are the kind words of support from the established scholars and churchmen who also endorsed the book. I would also like to thank John Angliss and SORCF for hosting the conference and treating us more regally than we deserved. At a personal level I am grateful to Brian Brewer, one of my undergraduate students, and also Virginia Snape, who both willingly offered their services in a research assistant capacity for one of my chapters and my ongoing research into Christian-state relations in the Holy Land. Finally, I thank my parents, Chris and Christine, for their valuable biblical instruction during my childhood years which I still continue to draw upon, and my wife Kay and our wonderful children (Isaac, Gabriella, Katrina, Dominiq and Esther) who, as always, patiently support my work and cheerily forgive me for working late hours and unwittingly missing family events.

Calvin L. Smith

Introduction

Israel and the Jews are of considerable interest to many Christians.
This is hardly surprising, given how the land of Israel is where
Jesus trod and Christianity emerged. Moreover, Israel is
mentioned or alluded to nearly 3000 times in the Bible, while as a
biblical theology theme it appears far more than many other
important themes in the Bible. Jesus and the Apostles were
Jewish, as was most of the early church, which was headquartered
in Jerusalem, the Jewish capital. Jews and Christians both draw on
the Old Testament, while much of the theology of Mosaic (though
not Rabbinic) Judaism serves as important background to
Christianity. Then, of course, there are the many Scriptures which
highlight the theological importance of Israel and the Jews. For
example, 'Salvation is from the Jews' (John 4:22); Zechariah
records God's declaration that ten Gentiles will take hold of the
tunic of a Jew saying, 'Let us go with you, for we have heard that
God is with you' (Zech 8:23); and the Apostle Paul introduces his
lengthy treatise on Israel by pointing out how the adoption as sons,
the glory, covenants, the giving of the law and promises belong to
the Jews, indeed the promised Messiah is Jewish (Rom 9:4-5).
Furthermore, the Prophets refer to Israel as both God's servant (Is
41:8-9, 44:1-3, 44:21, 49:3, Je 30:10, 46:27) and God's son (Hos
11:1, Ex 4:22). These and many other passages demonstrate just
how fully Israel is woven into the very historical and theological
fabric of the Bible and Christianity.

Christian Zionism, the view that modern Israel represents
God's restoration of His chosen people to the land, has existed
since the nineteenth century (though arguably one can trace the
notion that the Jews remain God's chosen people throughout
church history). Likewise, supercessionism (American spelling:
supersessionism) the view that the church has displaced, or
replaced Israel, also known as replacement theology, can also be
traced to the early church period. Yet the publication of various
books during the past two decades or so has witnessed a new

expression of supercessionism (hence the title of this book), specifically within Evangelicalism, which is deeply critical of modern Israel. It also tends, whether deliberately or unwittingly, to portray Christians who broadly believe God has not finished with the Jewish people, regardless of their theological tradition, as somehow fanatical and extreme, even heretical.

There are, of course, many Christians who regard Israel as a peripheral issue, even an irritating distraction, not least because getting to theological grips with this complex topic is costly both in time and the effort needed to reach a well-informed and biblically sustainable conclusion. I would agree Israel is not a test of orthodoxy; after all, we are saved through faith in Christ, not because we believe the Jews are God's chosen people. But as the above Scriptures indicate, neither is Israel a peripheral issue. It already divides the church along hermeneutical (biblical interpretation), systematic theology and practical theology lines. Moreover, as the current debate, which is beginning to trickle down to the church level, becomes increasingly polarised and bitter, inevitably this will push Israel up the theological ladder. For example, recently I came across anti-Israel and pro-Palestinian pamphlets being widely disseminated across a well-known, historic and traditionally conservative denomination.

Much more significant (and ominous) is how the issue of Israel has become a touch paper – how it is symptomatic – of a wider ideological conflict which appears to be brewing within Evangelicalism, certainly here in the United Kingdom but elsewhere too. It mirrors the debate currently being played out in British society concerning how to respond to Islam. Arguably, several of the more vocal and polemical supercessionists have crossed that line which separates legitimate criticism of Israel from an irrational, pathological hatred of the country. Such demonisation of the Jewish state, which comes perilously close to anti-Semitism, goes hand in hand with efforts by such to engage not only in Muslim-Christian dialogue, but also to promote a less confrontational and more sympathetic approach to Islam. In some cases, such an approach includes visits to Islamic centres, attending and speaking at meetings organised by Palestinian solidarity groups, and even visits to rogue Islamic states such as Iran, where these platforms are used to criticise Christians who support Israel and believe the Jews remain God's chosen people. Even Christians who do not openly support Israel but are nonetheless critical of Islam and what they perceive as an Islamist threat to Britain and the West are being singled out for criticism. A case in point is the recent situation involving Patrick Sookhdeo, a former Muslim convert to Christianity who leads the Barnabas Fund, a charity which speaks out on behalf of persecuted Christians worldwide, including those in Muslim lands. It appears he was recently criticised by some Christians who advocate a gentler, less confrontational approach to Islam, the result of which drew Sookhdeo to the attention of extremist Islamist bloggers. The issue has since been widely reported in the press, several blogs, and on the Barnabas Fund website.[1] Significantly, at least one of the Christians present at the meeting which allegedly criticised Sookhdeo's frank assessment of Islam is a well-known supercessionist who is highly critical of Israel and Christian Zionism. Thus we see how the Israel issue is increasingly symptomatic of a *wider* ideological struggle within British Evangelicalism. As such, it cannot be relegated to the periphery as an insignificant theological topic.

Ironically for the new supercessionists, many Evangelicals who were initially quite supportive of their position are becoming increasingly troubled by their radical stance and activities. I have met people within Evangelical academic circles who have

---

[1] For a narrative, see Melanie Phillips, 'Beware the New Axis of Evangelicals and Islamists', 4 March 2009. Available on the *Spectator* website at www.spectator.co.uk/the-magazine/features/3409686/beware-the-new-axis-of-evangelicals-and-islamists.thtml (last accessed 6 March 2009).

expressed such views, while recently the director of a theological college who originally leaned towards supercessionism explained to me how he had become uneasy with the rhetoric of certain high profile supercessionists, which actually led him to shift theologically in the other direction.

So how might Christians who generally reject supercessionism respond to this position in an effective and thoughtful manner? Many everyday Christians who, to varying degrees, take the view God has not finished with His people Israel are uneasy with an extreme form of Christian Zionism which takes an "Israel right or wrong" position. Such extremism is sometimes guilty of elevating Israel to dizzy heights, ignoring the fact it is a secular country led predominantly by secular politicians. Moreover, modern Israel is far from sinless (consider, for example, how some 20,000 or so abortions are carried out each year in Israel).[2] By ignoring Israel's flaws, some within the Christian Zionist camp almost engage in a form idolatry (or 'Israelolatry') of the Jewish state, guilty of propagating another form of replacement theology – replacing worship of God for worship of Israel. Instead, many intelligent lay Christians who by instinct support Israel are seeking a more balanced approach to the issue, which challenges and effectively refutes the new supercessionism, but which retains a solid theological basis and does not fall into the trap of Christian Zionist drum beating. There are, of course, some excellent academic treatments which roundly refute supercessionism (and so effectively that they are rarely discussed within the supercessionist literature). But such books are not always user-friendly or accessible to everyday Christians. Meanwhile, there are many popular books on the issue, but with the exception of some notable examples, pro-Israel popular books tend to lack a solid theological basis, relying on proof-texting or

---

[2] 'Israeli Government's Central Bureau of Statistics, 'Terminations of Pregnancy', (2006), see www1.cbs.gov.il/shnaton57/st03_19.pdf (last accessed 8 April 2009).

else spilling over into the very extreme Christian Zionism such thoughtful believers seek to avoid.

It was for these reasons King's Evangelical Divinity School (then Midlands Bible College and Divinity School) organised a weekend conference with a view to providing lay Christians with a range of theological resources aimed at equipping them to refute the new supercessionism objectively and effectively as God gave them opportunity. A series of papers were presented which, while academic in nature, were designed to be accessible to everyday Christians. These were then adapted in light of question and answer sessions and debates which followed, resulting in a book which has been pitched somewhere between the popular and academic levels.

When we organised this conference I purposefully brought together a group of lecturers and writers on the basis of their expertise and what they could bring to the seminar and this volume. But the contributors not only represent a range of theological disciplines, they also come from across the Evangelical theological spectrum. This is deliberate, challenging disingenuous efforts by several supercessionists to portray Christians who are broadly supportive of the view God has not finished with Israel somehow as a narrow, peripheral and fanatical segment within the church. So while all contributors are Evangelical, regarding the Bible as the inspired and authoritative word of God in all issues of faith and practice, and each rejects supercessionism, they are quite a disparate bunch, counting Reformed, Arminian, Dispensationalist, Charismatic and others among them. As such, each person contributes solely as an individual, responsible only for his own paper, and not necessarily endorsing the theological position from which the others come or the methodological approach I have taken in this book.

The book takes a standard academic approach to a theological issue, beginning with a study at the textual and word level, then working outwards and increasingly broadening its treatment, drawing on a range of theological disciplines with which to examine the topic. Thus, Andy Cheung explores Israel from a linguistic aspect, challenging those who argue that the word "Israel" in the New Testament, especially Romans 9-11, does not refer to ethnic Israel. In Chapter 2 I move beyond a textual approach to trace Israel as a biblical theology theme that encompasses the entire biblical witness (and, indeed, given how it features so prominently in biblical eschatology, beyond). Next, Jacob Prasch examines the issue from a hermeneutical (biblical interpretation) perspective, highlighting not only how a spiritualised interpretation of the Bible gives rise to supercessionism, but also demonstrating how a rejection of the Jewish root of the church is having a detrimental effect on the interpretation of Scripture in such circles as a whole. Stephen Vantassel then engages in a combined biblical and systematic theology approach, focusing on why, as a Calvinist, he believes Israel has a right to the land. This is followed by Howard Taylor's useful apologetic piece in support of Israel and the Jews. Next are two historical and political essays, the first by Paul Wilkinson, who provides readers with an historical survey of the British churchmen and Christian politicians who laid the foundations for an eventual Jewish homeland. His paper helps to dispel the myth so favoured by some supercessionists, which argues early Christian support for the establishment of a Jewish homeland was somehow the work of Zionist fanatics on the periphery of mainstream Evangelicalism. In fact, as Wilkinson demonstrates this is far from true, with many mainstream churchmen in nineteenth century Britain supporting the notion of a Jewish homeland. Meanwhile, my second essay, which is based on field work for a new book due for publication in 2010, challenges supercessionist allegations that Israel severely maltreats Arab Christians and is solely to blame for the exodus of Christians from the Holy Land. But I also highlight how the Jewish state is doing little to protect Messianic believers who face considerable opposition from religious Jews (indeed even passing laws which make the situation of Jewish believers in Jesus in Israel evermore precarious), thus challenging those Christian Zionists who take an 'Israel right or wrong' position. The book concludes with a chapter aimed at a practical outworking, in which Tony Pearce, whose church is located in Golders Green (a predominantly Jewish area in London) discusses issues arising out of and approaches to Jewish evangelism. By including this chapter my aim is not only to challenge the tendency (in practice, if not in word) of some supercessionists to fail to share the gospel with Jewish people, but also, just as importantly, to counter the doctrine espoused by some Christian Zionists of dual covenantalism (the view that postulates two ways of salvation, one for Jews through the Old Testament law, and another for Gentiles through Jesus Christ).

One final point. In an attempt to make this book as user-friendly as possible we have sought to avoid using too much technical language and from time to time include explanatory notes and definitions of theological terms in brackets and footnotes. Concerning terminology, in several chapters the terms Arab, Arab Israeli and Palestinian are used. These are not used interchangeably. The first refers to Arabs living anywhere in the Holy Land. Arab Israelis, on the other hand, live within the State of Israel and hold Israeli citizenship. Palestinians are those Arabs who live in the so-called Palestinian Territories – the West Bank and Jordan – who do not hold Israeli citizenship. Of course, the reality is not as simple as that (for example, many Arab Israelis identify themselves first and foremost as Palestinians, not all Palestinians are Muslims, and so on). As is inevitably the case in such a bitter conflict, whatever terms are used will be seized upon by one side or other as politically biased or insensitive. I recognise this cannot be helped. In fact, they are simply included here for practical reasons, for the necessary purpose of differentiating one group from another.

Calvin L. Smith
Broadstairs, Kent (6 March 2009)

CHAPTER 1

Who is the "Israel" of Romans 11:26?

Andy Cheung

For Evangelicals, sound theology and solid exegesis rest ultimately on a capacity to understand the underlying text. So while other Christian groups may prefer to base doctrines on historical patterns or particular authorities, Evangelicals insist upon correctly handling the written word. Accordingly, in approaching the question of the place of Israel in Christian theology, it is paramount that Evangelicals begin with some straightforward linguistics. The question at hand concerns the meaning of "Israel". This apparently simple question is not at all easy when one considers its usage in early Christian writings in general and the New Testament in particular. The term Israel in early Christian writings can include Gentiles, so we must be careful with it when we find it in Scripture. The goal in this chapter is to explore the meaning of "Israel" in Romans 11:26, a study that I suggest is of value to all Evangelicals, no matter which particular theological stance is held on the question of Israel.

Of particular concern in this paper is the usage of Israel in Romans 11:26, but before concentrating on this one verse we would be wise to consider a few relevant, necessary questions first:

- What does Israel mean in 11:25-26?
- What does Israel mean in Romans 9-11, and in Romans generally?
- What does Israel mean in the New Testament?
- What does Israel mean in early Christian literature?

We will begin in reverse order, but first some preliminary words on why this question matters at all.

Why is a study of Romans 11:26 important?
The verse is uniquely important in discussions concerning God's purpose for ethnic, historic Israel. Romans 11:26 reads, "And in this way all Israel will be saved" (ESV). Here we have a promise that there will be a future salvation for a group of people called Israel. But to whom does Israel refer in this verse? It either refers to historic, ethnic Israel or to a "new Israel" representing the Church of Gentiles and Jews.

If we take this verse to refer to ethnic Israel, it means we have a unique New Testament promise that there will be some kind of future salvation for all Jews (I will explore what is meant by the term "all" later). On the other hand, if Israel here is a synonym for the Church of Gentiles and Jews, then we have no such promise. Indeed, nowhere else in the New Testament is there a verse that potentially says as much as 11:26. Either God uniquely promises here a future salvation for ethnic Israel or no such promise exists at all. For this reason, Romans 11:26 demands closer study.

Is this question under debate?
For centuries, Christians have disagreed on the meaning of Israel in this verse. Modern scholarship seems to be moving towards a consensus that Israel in this verse refers to ethnic Jews: there are few modern commentaries on Romans that would deny this. However, there are still a number of scholars who believe that the term Israel refers to the Church of Gentiles and Jews.

Why engage in a linguistic study?
Most discussion of the place of Israel is necessarily theological. Questions such as 'Does Israel still have a place in God's purposes?' 'Does the land of Israel still belong to the Jews?' 'How do we understand the differences between the Old and New Testament with respect to Israel?' are all theological questions. But we cannot answer these without looking at the words of Scripture.

Theology, it must always be remembered, is a second-order task that follows exegetical and linguistic study.

WHAT DOES ISRAEL MEAN IN EARLY CHRISTIAN LITERATURE?

It is very clear that in early Christian literature, the term Israel was often used to refer to Christians generally, whether Jew or Gentile. We see this in Irenaeus, Clement of Alexandria, Theodore of Mopsuestia, Theodoret, Augustine, and Origen. The earliest definite application of the term Israel to Gentiles was by Justin Martyr (100–165) who wrote that the Church is 'the true spiritual Israel' in Dialogue 11.5, dated to around AD 150.

It is therefore beyond dispute that in the early Church, the term Israel is a valid synonym for the Church of Gentiles and Jews. But does this evidence require us to understand Israel in such ways in the New Testament? After all, the New Testament was completed at least 50 years before Justin Martyr's Dialogue. The other church fathers used the term Israel in later periods still. We may need to differentiate between the use of the word Israel in the early Church and its use in the New Testament. Peter Richardson for example has argued in his book, *Israel in the Apostolic Church*, that a new meaning was applied to Israel after the New Testament was written. In other words, Scripture would appear to be extremely careful and ethnically restrictive in its use of the term Israel.

If Richardson is right, then the evidence of the early Church is not directly relevant to understanding the meaning of Israel in Romans 11:26. Even if Israel is used as a synonym for the Gentile and Jewish church in early Christian history, it does not follow that the same pattern of usage is necessarily the case in the earlier documents of the New Testament. It may be wise to differentiate between the use of the word Israel by early church fathers and its use in the New Testament.

WHAT DOES ISRAEL MEAN IN THE NEW TESTAMENT?

In this section, we consider the term Israel in the New Testament. The word appears 68 times with the related word Israelite appearing nine times. There does not appear to be any doubt that the latter means a physical Jewish descendant so we focus our discussion on the term Israel only. The term appears as follows:

12 times in Matthew
2 times in Mark
12 times in Luke
4 times in John
15 times in Acts
11 times in Romans
1 time in 1 Corinthians
2 times in 2 Corinthians
1 time in Galatians
1 time in Ephesians
1 time in Philippines
3 times in Hebrews
3 times in Revelation

Most of the above instances undoubtedly refer to ethnic Israel, for example Luke 9:25 which reads, "there were many widows in Israel in the days of Elijah" (ESV). Such usage as found here poses no theological or lexical difficulty since the term can only refer to the historical land of Israel. But the situation is not so simple in certain New Testament verses whereupon the term Israel is used in a manner that may suggest a wider meaning. Indeed, four verses have sometimes been used to suggest that Israel can refer to the Church (made up of Gentiles and Jews). One of these verses of course is Romans 11:26, our key discussion point, but it will be fruitful and necessary for an examination of the other three verses, Galatians 6:16, 1 Corinthians 10:18 and Romans 9:6.

The use of the term Israel in Galatians 6:16

In this verse, scholars are divided over whether the apostle Paul uses the term Israel to refer to ethnic Israel or to the Church of Gentiles and Jews. Deciding which is the case is notoriously difficult because the Greek is ambiguous and could be understood either way. Most commentators make use of Paul's running theological themes in Galatians to determine the most likely answer but this in itself tends to raise different interpretations. We begin with a brief discussion of the original Greek.

The ESV translation of this verse reads, 'and as for all who walk by this rule, peace and mercy be upon them, and upon the Israel of God.' The English Standard Version (ESV) is an essentially literal translation and to an extent retains the ambiguity of the Greek. The apostle's blessing upon "all who walk by this rule" is understood by all sides of the debate to be a reference to the Church. But when the apostle subsequently follows this with the ambiguous "and upon the Israel of God", is he now addressing ethnic Israel, a separate group to the Church, or is he identifying the Church as the Israel of God?

The difference between these two is considerable: is Paul blessing just one group, the Israel of God made up of all Jewish and Gentile believers? Or is he placing a blessing upon two groups, the Church on the one hand, and ethnic Israel on the other? The difference between these two meanings is made clear when we consider two translations that adopt differing stances. Following are the respective renderings of the New Living Translation (NLT) and the Holman Christian Standard Bible (HCSB):

May God's peace and mercy be upon all who live by this principle; they are the new people of God. (NLT)

May peace be on all those who follow this rule, and mercy also be on the Israel of God! (HCSB)

What is the difference between the two? In the NLT, Israel is understood as the "new people of God" and they, the Church, are seen as the recipients of the apostle's blessing of 'peace and mercy'. In contrast, the HCSB has the apostle asking for peace upon the Church on the one hand, but then also mercy upon Israel. Since the HCSB separates the two groups, it is most likely that it considers Israel to be an ethnic entity separate from the Church.

Linguistic, Exegetical and Theological Analysis
We now turn to a brief discussion of the major viewpoints offered by commentators in their attempts to resolve this issue. The debate hinges on the Greek word for "and" (*kai*) in the phrase 'and also the Israel of God' (ESV). There are two possibilities for understanding this. The first approach is to take an appositional or explicative meaning in which Paul directs his words to one group only. The second approach has Paul extending his words to two separate groups and hence would give a meaning along the lines of, 'and additionally the Israel of God.' The first approach would produce a meaning such as, 'who are indeed the Israel of God.'

It is rather difficult to choose between the two, especially since the Greek is vague. Also, analysing the words is not helpful since "Israel of God" is found nowhere else in the New Testament or indeed any of the writings of Second Temple Judaism or later rabbinic writings. It is therefore unsurprising that most commentators seek to find a solution by looking at theological clues from the epistle itself. Alternatively, rhetorical analysis is often used. For example, one might be inclined to ask whether Paul would really have described his contemporary ethnic Jews as the Israel of God, especially since as a nation they largely rejected the Gospel. And as we shall see, there are some who believe that 1 Corinthians 10:18 ("Israel according to the flesh") reflects better Paul's preferred term for unbelieving Israel.[1] A counter argument

---

[1] The matter of the choice of words in 1 Corinthians 10:18 will be dealt with later.

to this can be found in Romans 11 where Paul asks the question 'has God rejected his people?' (ESV) The apostle has no apparent problem with referring to unbelieving ethnic Israel as "his people" and that being so, it seems reasonable for him to refer to them also as the Israel of God.

One approach that is sometimes taken is the matter of Paul's general theme in Galatians: it is thought possible to discern which meaning of Israel would be a contextually better fit. For example, if Paul has been arguing throughout the epistle that the promise of Abraham is for both Jews and Gentiles in Christ, would it not be somewhat strange for him at the end of the letter to suddenly separate his blessings between separate groups? Yet this seemingly valid argument is problematic because were Paul to identify Gentile Christians as Israel, he would therefore be conceding a major point of discussion between him and his Judaising opponents.

Such attempts to interpret the apostle's mind by trying to infer his likely intentions are largely unhelpful. Attempts to predict his likely train of argument produce alternative viewpoints none of which can be satisfactorily proven. It might be more fruitful to avoid rhetorical analyses and return to linguistic and exegetical approaches and here we are aided by one ancient text that may underlie the enigmatic phrase 'and upon the Israel of God.' The text in question is the 19th of the Jewish benedictions, particularly the "blessing of peace" of the Babylonian Recension which reads: 'bestow peace, happiness and blessing, grace and loving-kindness and mercy upon us and upon all Israel, your people'. This ancient prayer is of uncertain age but is generally considered to have been in existence at the time of Paul. The wording, especially in Greek, is similar enough to Galatians 6:16 that it or something similar to it may have been in Paul's mind.

Interestingly, Frank Matera, a professor of New Testament at the Catholic University of America, believes that the majority of commentators support this second view (that is, that Paul speaks to two different groups).[2] It is doubtful whether that is true generally across Church history but it may well be the case that in recent years there has been a gradual move towards it by Greek scholars.

How does the second approach deal with the words, 'and as for all who walk by this rule, peace and mercy be upon them, and upon the Israel of God'? The first group is clearly the Church (containing Jews and Gentiles) and they are addressed as 'all who walk by this rule' while 'the Israel of God' are understood as a second group altogether. But it is not enough to simply conclude that it refers to Israel for we ought to be more specific.

Seeking a more specific definition of "Israel"
If we grant that Israel refers to ethnic Jews, there remains further consideration: are they unbelieving Jews? Believing Jews? Or a mixture of both? The preference among scholars is to understand the verse as referring to Jewish Christians[3] but I prefer to understand the verse as referring to unbelieving Jews. The HCSB translation quoted above is a satisfactory rendering of the Greek and importantly, it makes exegetical and theological sense for Paul to pray for "peace" upon Christians yet "mercy" for unbelieving Jews. After all, it would be unnecessary to extend a separate blessing upon believing Jews when they are already accounted for in Paul's initial prayer for 'all who follow this rule.' The second, separate blessing should be seen as directed to another group, non-Christians, and specifically Jewish non-Christians. There is also good reason for Paul to pray for *mercy* upon his unbelieving fellow Jews. Consider his anguish over Jewish unbelievers in

---

[2] Frank J. Matera, *Galatians, Sacra Pagina 9* (Collegeville, MA: Liturgical Press, 1992), 232.
[3] See for instance, Robert Keith Rapa, "Galatians" in Tremper Longman III and David E. Garland, eds. *The Expositor's Bible Commentary Revised Edition, volume 11 Romans-Galatians* (Grand Rapids, MI: Zondervan, 2008), 638-639.

Romans 9:1-5, but especially these verses from Romans 11:30-32 where Paul also speaks of the *mercy* that is due to unbelieving Israel:

> [11:30] *For just as you were at one time disobedient to God but now have received mercy because of their disobedience,* [31] *so they too have now been disobedient in order that by the mercy shown to you they also may now receive mercy.* [32] *For God has consigned all to disobedience, that he may have mercy on all.*

The use of the term Israel in 1 Corinthians 10:18

This verse occasionally solicits comment because it could imply that there are two Israels: a fleshly Israel, and a spiritual Israel. This idea springs from Paul's words, 'consider Israel according to the flesh' which could be taken to mean there is such a thing as an 'Israel according to the Spirit.'[4] But these words occur in the midst of discussion on idolatry and Paul's intention is to discuss the Israel of ancient times and although the assertion by Fee is possible, it is more likely that *kata sarka* (according to the flesh) refers to earthly descent, and is therefore not about spirituality. Paul is not describing an unbelieving Jewish group but rather an ethnic group of descendants. That is how the ESV understands it by rightly translating, 'Consider the people of Israel'. There does not seem to be any linguistic or exegetical reason for inferring the existence of an 'Israel according to the Spirit.' Furthermore, there is also no reason to suppose that 'Israel according to the flesh' requires also an 'Israel according to the Spirit', a term that is found nowhere in the New Testament.

---

[4] This is the view of Gordon Fee, *The First Epistle to the Corinthians* (Grand Rapids, MI: W.B. Eerdmans, 1987), 470f.

The use of the term Israel in Romans 9:6

We turn now to a much quoted verse which seems to imply that the term Israel can be used to refer to Gentiles as well as Jews. The ESV translates thus: 'But it is not as though the word of God has failed. For not all who are descended from Israel belong to Israel.' There is no disagreement with the first usage of the term Israel in this passage: all are agreed that it concerns ethnic Israel. But what does the second Israel mean? There are two possibilities: either it means the Church or it means a spiritual remnant within Israel. If we paraphrase the statement with these two alternative ideas in mind we must choose between either:

1) Not all who are descended from Israel *belong to the Church.*
2) Not all who are descended from Israel *belong to the spiritual remnant within Israel.*

The difference between these two is significant. The first option *widens* the meaning of Israel from ethnic Jews to the entire Church of Gentiles and Jews. The second option *narrows* the meaning of Israel from ethnic Jews to a spiritual remnant within Israel.[5] There are two exegetical reasons for preferring the second interpretation.

Firstly, the meaning of Israel in this verse must be tied to the use of the term Israelites in 9:4-5. These two verses are part of the opening statements that Paul begins to explain in 9:6. In other words, there is a direct, indissoluble connection between 9:6 and 9:4-5. Moreover, it is clear from the context that the Israelites of 9:4-5 refers to ethnic Jews. Indeed, the word Israelite appears nine times in the New Testament and is never used for Gentiles. Since the term Israelite is restricted in its usage to ethnic Jews, it is therefore more likely for Israel in 9:6 to be likewise restrictive.

---

[5] Scholars are divided on this and among those who prefer the first option are N. T. Wright and Eugene Nida. Among those who prefer the second are Thomas Schreiner, Douglas Moo and Charles Cranfield.

Secondly, 9:7-13 focuses on God's winnowing process whereby through successive generations of Abraham, Isaac and Jacob, God narrows his chosen people to a spiritual remnant. This winnowing, a theme of the remnant, fits perfectly with the idea that Israel in 9:6 refers to a spiritual remnant of Israel within the larger ethnic group of Jews generally. Hence, 9:6 teaches that not every Jew is a part of God's selected remnant of believing Jews.

WHAT DOES ISRAEL MEAN IN ROMANS 9-11, AND IN ROMANS GENERALLY?

A few brief remarks on the theme of Romans may be useful. The purpose behind Paul's writing of the great epistle is disputed which is unsurprising given that the apostle does not explain his purposes. A steady stream of theories have been proposed over the years[6] but in my view the best course of reasoning is one that follows approximately a path originally struck by F. C. Baur[7] in 1876 who proposed that Gentile/Jewish divisions at the church in Rome necessitated Paul's desire to set right a growing and dangerous disharmony in a congregation that was splitting along ethnic lines. There is insufficient space in this article to pursue this idea but I do think that the disunity between Gentile and Jewish believers is one of the main causes of Paul's writing of Romans and especially chapters 9-11.

The relevance of this to our present discussion is that if part of Paul's reason for writing Romans emanates from a need to resolve conflicts between Gentile and Jewish Christians, it follows that 11:26 is just one important part of an ongoing discussion and

---

[6] The best single volume collection of essays is K. P. Donfried, *The Romans Debate – Expanded Edition* (Peabody, MA: Hendrickson Publishers, 1991).
[7] F. C. Baur, *Paul the Apostle of Jesus Christ, His Life and Work, His Epistles and His Doctrine. A Contribution to a Critical History of Primitive Christianity* (London: Williams and Norgate, 1876).

hence we should avoid isolating it from the rest of the epistle. In Romans, the word Israel appears 11 times and Israelite two times. The only occurrence that is debated is 11:26 but if the theme of Israel is so important throughout the letter, why would Paul adopt a different meaning in this one verse? It seems more likely that in a letter dominated by Gentile and Jewish relations, and especially in the section of the epistle (chapters 9-11) that focuses particularly on these themes, the apostle would not modify his normal usage of the term Israel.

One other item is worthy of remark at this point. The word Jew appears 11 times in the epistle and I consider every instance to refer to an ethnic Israelite. But Romans 2:28-29 is sometimes interpreted to describe a 'true Jew', a Christian who may be Gentile or Jewish. The pertinent verses are as follows:

> [2:28] *For no one is a Jew who is merely one outwardly, nor is circumcision outward and physical.* [29] *But a Jew is one inwardly, and circumcision is a matter of the heart, by the Spirit, not by the letter. His praise is not from man but from God.* (ESV)

All interpreters agree on the following: Paul argues that mere circumcision does not make someone a 'true Jew.' True spirituality is a matter of the heart and not a matter of outward law keeping. So far so good but the error often made is to assume that anybody, Gentile or Jew, who finds faith in Christ is therefore a Jew inwardly. But this is not what Paul means. Rather, he is restricting the traditional definition of Jew to an ethnic Israelite who has faith in Christ. So instead of *widening* the meaning of Jew to embrace all Gentile believers, the apostle is *narrowing* the meaning of Jew to only those Israelites who have found faith in Christ. The approach to this verse is similar to that taken in Romans 9:6 where I argued that the meaning of Israel was not being widened to include Gentiles, but narrowed to a spiritual remnant within Israel.

WHAT DOES ISRAEL MEAN IN 11:25-26?

Having laid the groundwork, we come now to our main subject, the meaning of Israel in Romans 11:26 which is best considered by looking also at the preceding verse 11:25. The link between the two verses is clear from the words 'and in this way' at the beginning of verse 26 and which demonstrate the connection between the two verses.[8]

> *Lest you be wise in your own conceits, I want you to understand this mystery, brothers: a partial hardening has come upon Israel until the fullness of the Gentiles has come in. And in this way all Israel will be saved.* (ESV)

How should we understand the term Israel in the expression 'all Israel will be saved'? It is occasionally suggested that here the term Israel refers to the Church[9] and is therefore a promise that God will save all Christians. But as we shall see, it is far more likely that the term Israel excludes Gentiles.

The immediate context of these two verses is the theme of Israel's ingrafting. In Romans 11:17-24, Paul writes about the natural branches being grafted back into their own olive tree. Accordingly we ought to interpret verse 25 against the backdrop of this metaphor of wild and cultivated olive tree: a discourse that nobody doubts is concerned with ethnic Israel and Gentiles. Moreover, verse 25 also references ethnic Israel by discussing their partial hardening. Once again, there is no doubt among any commentator that verse 25 refers only to ethnic Israel. When we

---

[8] A few translations treat verse 26 as beginning a new sentence but this is most unlikely. The standard Greek editions, UBS[4] and NA[27]connect it with verse 25, a view shared by the majority of Greek exegetes.

[9] Most recently claimed by Christopher R. Bruno, 'The Deliverer from Zion: The Source(s) and Function of Paul's Citation in Romans 11:26-27', *Tyndale Bulletin*, 59.1, 2008, 119-134.

consider verse 26 against this, we can isolate three distinct clauses between the two verses:

11:25 A partial hardening has come upon Israel
*   until the fullness of the Gentiles has come in*
26 and in this manner all Israel will be saved.

It would be linguistically naive to assume that Paul changes the meaning of Israel upon commencing verse 26. The strong words of John Murray do not seem to be an overstatement:

> *It should be apparent from both the proximate and less proximate contexts in this portion of the epistle that it is exegetically impossible to give to 'Israel' in this verse any other denotation than that which belongs to the term throughout this chapter. There is the sustained contrast between Israel and the Gentiles ... What other denotation could be given to Israel in the preceding verse? It is of ethnic Israel Paul is speaking and Israel could not possibly include Gentiles. In that event the preceding verse would be reduced to absurdity and since verse 26 is a parallel or correlative statement the denotation of 'Israel' must be the same as in verse 25.[10]*

To Whom Does "All Israel" Refer?

The previous section demonstrated that "all Israel" is best understood as representing ethnic Israel but we need to be more specific. For instance, by "all Israel" do we mean every individual Jew? Or do we mean the nation as a whole generally? There are three possibilities:

---

[10] John Murray, *The Epistle to the Romans, the English Text with Introduction, Exposition and Notes.* Volume 2 (Grand Rapids, MI: Eerdmans, 1965), 96.

1. All Israel refers to every Jewish Christian.
2. All Israel refers to every individual Israelite.
3. All Israel refers to ethnic Israel as a whole.

The first option is possible but may be discarded because such a statement would be redundant. In effect it would leave Paul saying that all Jews who have been saved will be saved. Such a statement is unnecessary and thereby renders this option unlikely. The second option has attracted some considerable support[11] for it enables the word "all" to be taken literally, even if this might pose considerable soteriological questions.

But there are two reasons for preferring the third option by which "all Israel" refers to ethnic Israel as a whole. Paul is not saying that every individual Jew will one day be saved but rather that the nation generally, as an ethnic identity, will find salvation in the Messiah. The fact is that the Greek term behind "all Israel" is not the most obvious way of referring to every individual Jew. Better options exist which might produce English equivalents such as "all Israelites" or "all Jews" but as it stands "all Israel" has an ambiguity evident as much in English as in Greek. As a phrase, 'all Israel will be saved' is not strong enough to indicate every living individual.

Secondly, there is a biblical basis for understanding "all Israel" to mean ethnic Israel as a whole. For this, we must turn to the Septuagint, an ancient translation of the Hebrew Bible into Greek. Its precise date of emergence is disputed but certainly arrived long before the New Testament which quotes from it frequently. Undoubtedly, Greek speaking Jews (such as the apostle Paul) were acquainted with it and their vocabulary was shaped by it.

---

[11] Such as Robert Jewett, *Romans : A Commentary (Hermeneia, a Critical and Historical Commentary on the Bible)* (Minneapolis, MN: Fortress Press, 2007), 701-702.

In the Septuagint, we find some examples of "all Israel" which refer not to every individual Israelite but to the people generally, as a whole. In Numbers 16 there is the description of Korah's rebellion where a group of rebels turned against Moses and Aaron by challenging their authority. But their evil actions brought upon God's judgement and the ground swallowed them up. Then in 16:34 it says that "all Israel who were around them fled their cries." The point here is that the people as a whole, as a group, sought refuge from the disaster. It is not stating that every individual Jew fled but merely those "who were around them".

Another example can be found in Joshua 7. Following the defeat at Ai, Achan is discovered to have sinned against the Lord by stealing possessions and defaming God's glory. In the ensuing judgement, we read that 'all Israel stoned him with stones' (Joshua 7:25). It is of course unlikely that every single living Israelite took part in the actual stoning. Rather, it was the actions of a representative group of Israelites, acting on behalf of Israel as a whole.

A final example of a generic "all Israel" can be found in 2 Samuel 16 which describes the events following Absalom's revolt. At one point he takes his father's concubines onto the roof of the palace whereupon we read, 'And Absalom went into his father's concubines in the sight of all Israel' (2 Samuel 16:22). Once again there are the words "all Israel" and again it does not literally mean every single Israelite. Rather, it means that Israel generally, as a corporate nation, witnessed Absalom's taking of his father's concubines.

Accordingly, when Romans 11:26 states that all Israel will be saved, it is best understood that ethnic Israel will as a whole receive salvation even if the promise is not extended to every single individual Jew.

CONCLUSION

The following points are crucial in our understanding of the meaning of Israel in Romans 11:26. Firstly, the term Israel is ambiguous in early Christian literature which at times uses the term as a synonym for the Church, but other times reserves the usage for ethnic Israelites only. But although this practice is apparent among second century writers and beyond, the New Testament appears to be far more restrictive in its usage of the term.

There are four New Testament verses in which the term Israel appears to have a meaning that includes Gentiles. This is certainly the view of a number of commentators but close analysis suggests that at best, such interpretation is uncertain and it is more likely that these four passages restrict the meaning of Israel to ethnic Jews alone. The weight of evidence suggests that every single instance of the term Israel in the New Testament refers to the ethnic nation alone. That being the case, Israel 11:26 should be seen as a declaration that God will one day bring salvation to "all Israel", a term that refers to the nation generally, as a whole.

CHAPTER 2

Biblical Theology and the Modern State of Israel[1]

Calvin L. Smith

Biblical theology is notoriously difficult to define, consisting of quite diverse meanings and methods at different stages in the field of biblical studies.[2] At its most basic, biblical theology focuses on the unifying central story (the technical term is 'metanarrative') which runs through the Bible. Thus, biblical theology contributes to hermeneutics by drawing on the 'big picture' to interpret the Bible's various component parts, rather than simply limiting interpretation to the study of the Bible's books and texts. Another (related) way of doing biblical theology is to establish and trace unifying themes throughout the Bible, for example, sacrifice, redemption, the people of God, and so on.

Israel is a key biblical theme drawing on both these methods. As well as an important biblical theology theme in its own right (Israel is mentioned or alluded to some 3000 times in both Testaments), Israel plays a key role in the Bible's central story of redemption. Old Testament Israel is the people of God with whom He makes a covenant, reveals His laws, and ultimately through whom He sends a Saviour, a Jewish Messiah. Indeed, few

---

[1] A version of this paper was originally presented to a joint session of the Biblical Theology/Religion, Culture and Communication/Ethics and Social Theology groups on 5 July 2007 during the annual Tyndale Fellowship Study Groups Conference, Cambridge. Several useful comments made during the ensuing discussion are reflected here. This paper also appears in the *Evangelical Review of Society and Politics* 3.1 (2009).
[2] For a useful academic treatment of biblical theology, consider Craig Bartholomew, Mary Healy, Karl Moller and Robin Parry, eds. *Out of Egypt: Biblical Theology and Biblical Interpretation.* Scripture and Hermeneutics Series. Volume 5 (Bletchley: Paternoster, 2004).

Evangelicals would dispute Israel represented the revelatory vehicle for God's plan of redemption. Where supercessionists and their opponents disagree is whether God *continues* to recognise and have a plan for Israel now that His salvific plan has been revealed.

The view that Israel's theological purpose has been superceded is referred to by the theologian R. Kendall Soulen as 'structural supercessionism'. He traces how this position arose within church history by some theologians downplaying certain aspects of the Bible's metanarrative[3] (he prefers the term 'canonical narrative') while elevating others.[4] In effect, the Bible's central narrative can be reduced to four key events: creation, the Fall, Christ's work at the cross, and the end (or consummation) of the age. If you think about it, all the Bible's disparate components ultimately fit in with and are subordinate to these four events. But Soulen notes how, by focusing almost wholly on the Fall and God's response (Calvary), the other two events (creation and consummation) are downplayed. Moreover, by focusing on the New Testament story of Calvary as the zenith of God's eternal plan, the Old Testament is relegated in importance, and of course with it the role of Israel. Meanwhile, relegating the consummation of the age (which is, in fact, when the Bible narrative climaxes and ends and eternity begins) downplays the many eschatological passages in which Israel features so strongly. Indeed, it is no coincidence that those churches who relegate Israel's role also tend to downplay the issue of eschatology.

Supercessionists also focus on other biblical theology themes to support their position, notably who owns the land. They note this was an important Old Testament theme but it is barely mentioned in the New Testament. Thus, it is maintained the land is superceded, spiritualised and replaced with a new kingdom of God

---

[3] Grand, central narrative or structure around which the Bible is built.
[4] R. Kendall Soulen, *The God of Israel and Christian Theology* (Minneapolis, MN: Fortress Press, 1996).

which spans the whole earth, and Christians arguing for Israel's right to the land are theologically wrong. I will not deal with the land theme here as Stephen Vantassel challenges this view eloquently and persuasively in Chapter 4. Another biblical theme employed by replacementists is Israel's treatment of the alien, which I discuss briefly and challenge below.

This chapter, however, seeks to move beyond these and explore another biblical theology theme which is rarely discussed, namely, the house of Israel. After outlining and testing the viability of the house of Israel as a biblical theology theme, I offer some concluding thoughts which, together with my closing remarks in Chapter 7, are designed to offer some practical steps to help us approach the Middle East crisis thoughtfully and objectively.

THE HOUSE OF ISRAEL AS A BIBLICAL THEME

In the Old Testament the theme of Israel is so well developed we need hardly dwell on it here. Israel was God's chosen people, entrusted with a land to reside in and serve Him. Yet though the land certainly helped define Israel,[5] it must be recognised that land ownership is but *one* dimension of nationhood. After all, biblical Israel survived as a nation during exile and occupation, while for example today, despite the absence of an independent Kurdistan, the Kurds claim nationhood. So while the geographical dimension is important, nationhood comprises much more than this and such was the case for biblical Israel.

More important for Israel's identity was the religious dimension. She was chosen to be in a covenantal relationship with God, a national congregation[6] and a nation of priests (Ex 19:6), unique in history because of her relationship with God (Deut 4:34, 2 Sam 7:23). Israel enjoyed a unique, dynamic relationship with

---

[5] Indeed, the bequest of the land remains a tenet of Judaism to this day.
[6] There are numerous references and allusions to the `congregation of Israel' in the Old Testament.

the God of Abraham, Isaac, and Jacob, who loved, guided, instructed, and disciplined her. Not only this, but as Pierre Grelot demonstrates, history is central to the Israelite religious experience.[7] History is a vital dimension of any nation's self-identity. In Israel's case, however, history and religious self-consciousness were inextricably intertwined and indivisible, a symbiosis which formed a central defining feature of Israelite national identity. This, in turn, shaped and drove Israel's cultural identity, which is another important aspect of nationhood.

Aside from these religious, historical, cultural, and geographical features, there is also an ethnic dimension to Israelite nationhood. Israel was to be a distinctly *Jewish* nation. That is not to say, however, this precluded outsiders from joining the house of Israel.[8] God loved and welcomed the alien into the house of Israel (Deut 10:18-19). Aliens were permitted to join Israel, were granted full rights and privileges, and strict instructions were laid down concerning their fair treatment.[9] In fact, in God's eyes there was to be no difference between the alien and Israelite (Lev 24:22, Num 15:14-16).

Several supercessionists have developed a biblical theology theme of alien inclusion to challenge the view that modern Israel remains the people of God.[10] They state that because Israel today mistreats Palestinians, the nation is disobeying the Torah's commandments concerning alien inclusion and as such she is no

---

[7] Pierre Grelot, *The Language of Symbolism: Biblical Theology, Semantics, and Exegesis* (Peabody, MA: Hendrickson, 2006), 103ff.

[8] As Matthew's genealogy notes, aliens such as Tamar, Rahab, and Ruth became not only full participant members of the congregation of Israel, but they are also listed as direct ancestors of the Jewish Messiah.

[9] Consider Lev 23:22, Num 35:15, Deut 10:19, 14:29, 24:17, 24:19-21, 26:13, 27:19, Ezek 22:7 and Jer 7:6.

[10] See Gary Burge, *Whose Land? Whose Promise? What Christians Are Not Being Told About Israel and the Palestinians* (Cleveland, Ohio: Pilgrim Press, 2003), 88-93, and Colin Chapman, *Whose Promised Land?* (Oxford: Lion, 1983, 2002), 204ff.

longer in covenant with God as His chosen people. Leaving aside how their own leaders and the wider Arab must shoulder considerable responsibility for the current situation of Palestinians,[11] or how pro-Palestinian Christians taking this position shoot themselves in the foot by unwittingly suggesting the Palestinians are aliens in a land which rightly belongs to Israel, the argument of alien inclusion fails the biblical theology test by virtue of its selectiveness of texts. Indeed, it is undeniable from the Old Testament texts cited that God loved deeply and cared greatly for the aliens within biblical Israel. Crucially, however, this alien inclusion into the house of Israel was a *reciprocal,* covenantal arrangement, dependent upon various requirements and religious observances by the alien.[12] In short, aliens who joined the congregation of Israel were to leave their people, nation, and religion and become, to all intents and purposes, an Israelite, as so eloquently expressed in those words of Ruth the Moabitess to her mother-in-law Naomi, 'Your people shall be my people, and your God, my God' (Ruth 1:16). Thus we see an Old Testament type, or allusion, of a Gentile church being grafted in to Israel, as discussed by Paul in Romans 11:13-24 (cf Eph 2:11-14).

Hence, appeals to this aspect of the Mosaic Law to condemn modern Israel's relationship with the Palestinians ignore the reciprocity element and as such are theologically problematic. The

---

[11] This issue has been discussed widely in the ongoing debate surrounding the Middle East crisis. For an example of a recent newspaper article exploring the issue, see Catherine Philp, 'Palestinians dumped by road in no-man's land, ignored by all' in *The Times* (6 February 2009). The article is also available online at www.timesonline.co.uk/tol/news/world/iraq/article5671797.ece   (last accessed 9 February 2009).

[12] For example, the alien was expected to observe certain religious and other laws (Ex 12:19, Lev 16:29, 17:12, 17:15, 18:26, 24:16, Num 19:10, Deut 26:11, 31:12, Ezek 47:23). Moreover, if he was to become a member of the congregation and participate in the Passover feast (a key aspect of being an Israelite), he was to be circumcised (Ex 12:48-49, Num 9:14). Certain religious observances were expected not just from the alien, but also the sojourner (Ex 12:45, 20:10, Deut 5:1).

Palestinians are *not* in a reciprocal covenant – whether religious or political – with Israel today, while the Old Testament is equally clear that where any member of the house of Israel, whether an alien or Jew, not abiding by the covenant was to be excommunicated (Num 15:30). Moreover, such arguments also completely ignore how modern Israel's relationship with West Bank and Gazan Palestinian Arabs differs considerably from that with its 1.4 million or so Israeli Arabs (i.e. Arabs with full Israeli citizenship living within Israel's nationally recognised borders, as opposed to Palestinian Arabs in what the U.N. regards as occupied territory). These are the Arabs who, by formally accepting Israeli citizenship, have indeed come into a covenant of sorts with modern Israel.[13] Reciprocity is extended in the form of Israeli Arabs being permitted to vote, form political parties, sit in the Knesset, lobby parliament, take their grievances to the Israeli courts and, as the Haredim (Ultra-Orthodox Jews), are exempt from compulsory military service. To be sure, Israel's relations with its Arab citizens are not perfect.[14] For example, Israel often does not extend the same amount of state funding to Arab compared with Jewish areas, while for their part some Arab Israeli leaders express more loyalty to their own country's enemies (which has become an electoral issue during the Israeli general

---

[13] Recently, however, some Israeli Arab leaders have become increasingly vocal in their denunciation of the Jewish state. This has lead one right-wing Israeli politician, Avigdor Lieberman, during the general election held at the time of writing, to call for the introduction of an oath of allegiance, with citizenship being stripped from those who refuse (for example, see Damien McElroy and Dina Kraft, 'Former nightclub bouncer Lieberman set to hold balance of power after Israeli elections' in *The Daily Telegraph* (27 January 2008), online edition: www.telegraph.co.uk/news/worldnews/middleeast/israel/4347827/Forme r-nightclub-bouncer-Lieberman-set-to-hold-balance-of-power-after-Israeli-elections.html, last accessed 9 February 2009).

[14] That is not to say all these rights are necessarily always exercised unfettered, though Israeli Arabs arguably face problems because some reject the legitimacy of their own state.

election being held at the time of writing). Nonetheless, there *is* a covenant and reciprocity of sorts between Israeli Arabs and the state in a democratic Israel which extends more rights to its Arab citizens than many autocratic Arab states. Clearly, then, the claims by some supercessionists that Israel does not practice alien inclusion fail not only theologically, but also in practice.

Getting back to the main point concerning what constitutes nationhood, ethnicity represented an important dimension of Israelite identity and nationhood. Retention of a distinct Jewishness (but not to the point of exclusivity, also allowing aliens to join the national congregation) ensured biblical Israel retained its unique identity.[15] When in the Bible Israel mingled *en masse* with outsiders, they are condemned because such activity diluted Israel's religious identity and enticed the nation to serve foreign gods (for example, Ezra 9:2).

In summary, then, ancient Israel's nationhood was defined by a unique relationship with God that shaped its very history, together with a cultural, geographical, and finally, an ethnic dimension (though the outsider who abided by the covenant was also welcomed). Thus, Israel practiced an integrationist rather than a multicultural model. During New Testament times, the nation exhibits these same traits. The Jews still regarded themselves as a nation,[16] as does the apostle Paul.[17]. The religious dimension is strongly evident, as is Israel's ethnicity (Acts 7:19).

---

[15] Several supercessionists argue that a Jewish state is by its very nature racist, thus rendering modern Israel theologically in error. Yet today (much like in Old Testament times) Israel's Law of Return permits Jewish proselytes (i.e. *not* ethnically Jewish) to make *aliyah* (emigrate to Israel). Moreover, citizenship is automatically extended to *non*-Jewish spouses, children, and grandchildren, while the inclusion of Ethiopian and Yemenite Jews demonstrates that Jewishness moves beyond ethnicity and Israel is *far* from racist. For details of the Law of Return see the document posted on the Jewish Agency for Israel website at www.jewishagency.org/JewishAgency/English/Aliyah/Aliyah+Info/The +Law+of+Return/The+Law+of++Return.htm (accessed 16 July 2007).

[16] For example, Lk 7:5, 23:2, Jn 11:48, 50, Acts 10:22.

At this stage we must consider two questions. First, are these features of nationhood present within the modern state of Israel? Even a superficial perusal indicates this is so. Despite being a secular country, Judaism underpins much of Israeli society. This tension between the secular and sacred means there is no written Israeli constitution. Religious political parties such as Shas (a Sephardic party) and United Torah Judaism (Ashkenazi) are often kingmakers in Israeli politics, securing special laws (much to the annoyance of secular Jews) which exempt Haredi men from military service and finance their studies at *yeshiva*.[18] There is no civil marriage in Israel. Meanwhile, Jerusalem is deeply conservative and religious, unlike hedonist Tel Aviv. In the Haredi *Meah Sharim* neighbourhood you drive a car on the Sabbath or bare your arms and legs at your peril. Much of the settler activity is driven by Ultra-Orthodox theology. Even non-fundamentalist Jews follow dietary laws, celebrate the Sabbath, and draw strongly on their religious heritage and biblical history. Despite its cosmopolitan nature, Israel projects a strongly Jewish identity, while proselytisation is unusual and conversion to Judaism difficult. Indeed, the return of Palestinian refugees is such a sensitive issue precisely because it threatens to dilute the Jewish state.[19]

So despite secularism, atheism, and behaviour from some quarters that blatantly flouts the Mosaic Law, nonetheless much of modern Israel exhibits the features of biblical nationhood. Surely, this zeal for the religion, history, traditions and God of biblical Israel suggests to a degree how we as Christians should view modern Israel, or rather, a large segment of it. Christian Zionists do well to note Israel is a secular country which counts non- (or

---

[17] Acts 24:2, 17, 26:4, 28:19.

[18] Religious schools for the study of the Torah and Talmud.

[19] As does Israeli Arab demography, much like the higher Catholic birth rates compared with those of the Protestant community in Northern Ireland.

even anti-) religious elites among its numbers. But within that country is a bloc which demonstrates all the dimensions of the people of God from Old Testament times.

This leads us to the second question: what biblical evidence is there to indicate Israel still retains a special and unique place in God's eyes, both before *and after* Christ instituted a new covenant?

Jesus' ministry amazed the people (Mt 7:28) and His miracles caused them to glorify the God of Israel (Mt 15:31, Jn 12:13). He told the Syro-Phoenician woman He was sent only to the lost sheep of the house of Israel (Mt 15:24), instructing His disciples to do likewise (Mt 10:5-6). Jesus also expressed great love and tenderness towards Jerusalem (Mt 23:37, Lk 13:34). Meanwhile Yahweh is known as the Lord God of Israel (eg Lk 1:68), Jesus is the consolation of Israel (Lk 2:25), and Simeon refers to Him as the glory of God's people Israel (Lk 2:32). Given this ministry to and love for Israel it is arguably a hermeneutical stretch always to spiritualise or allegorise the term "Israel",[20] as well as theologically problematic to dismiss the house of Israel as somehow no longer important to God after many centuries of loving and caring for her prior to New Testament times. More problematic is the suggestion that somehow Israel has been (almost begrudgingly) attached to a Gentile Church, almost as an afterthought, when in fact Paul declares that it was Gentiles who were separated from the commonwealth of Israel and afar from God (Eph 2:12-13), and that God broke off some of the branches of unbelieving Israel so that we, a wild olive, might be grafted in and become partakers of the rich olive tree (Rom 11:17). The root supports the Gentile church, not the other way around (Rom

---

[20] Arguably, the word "Israel" in the New Testament (with the oft cited exception of the first reference to Israel in Rom 9:6, and the 'the Israel of God' in Gal 6:16 cf the false Judaisers, but see Andy Cheung's comprehensive discussion in Chapter 1) always denotes an ethnic entity. Surely, then, the onus is on those who believe so to demonstrate how the New Testament use of the word "Israel" has shifted from an ethnic to an allegorised definition, rather than the other way around.

11:18). That there are apostles to both Jew and Gentile in the book of Acts suggests Israel has not been dispossessed of her heritage.[21] Meanwhile, when the apostles asked the resurrected Jesus if he was about to restore the kingdom to Israel (Acts 1:6), he did not correct them to the effect there would be no such restoration, simply that it was not for them to know the times and epochs.

Paul has a great deal to say about Israel. We know at times he observed Israelite religious traditions (Acts 24:17, 26:4). While he states there is no difference between those Jews and Gentiles who are *already* in Christ Jesus,[22] nonetheless Paul regularly differentiates between Jew and Gentile, whether stating (and demonstrating) that the Gospel is to be taken to the Jew first (eg Rom 1:16), declaring that the Jew will suffer tribulation first (Rom 2:9), and even wishing it were possible for himself to be cut off from Christ for the sake of his Jewish kinsmen (Rom 9:1-3). Romans 9 to 11 is a major passage for consideration.[23] In the first five verses of this text Paul appeals to every one of the religious, historical, cultural, and ethnic dimensions of Israelite nationhood discussed above, and later explicitly refers to the Israelite nation (Rom 10:19). Thus, this passage relates to the election of a *nation* (expressed through Jacob over Esau, the father of the Edomites) rather than *individuals.* Paul maintains God has not rejected His people (Rom 11:1), that only unbelieving branches are stripped off to make way for outsiders to be grafted in. So whereas replacement theology claims the Church *replaces* Israel, the Church in fact is *joined* to Israel. Paul then warns the transplanted branches not to become arrogant, saying God is quite capable of removing them and re-grafting the old branches. Again, we are back to our discussion of the alien joining and entering into

---

[21] Pierre Grelot makes a similar point in *Language of Symbolism*, 142.

[22] See Rom 10:12, 1 Cor 12:13, Gal 3:28, and Col 3:11.

[23] Rom 9:1–5 clearly indicates Paul is referring to ethnic, rather than a spiritualised Israel here, and even Colin Chapman accepts that most of this passage relates to the Jewish people (*Whose Promised Land?* 245).

covenant with the house of Israel, such as Ruth, and in this instance, the Gentile church.

The thrust of Paul's entire argument is found at the end of Romans 11, where he discusses how Israel has been used to bring salvation to the world (thus echoing Old Testament passages alluding to universalism[24]). He explains how salvation, which emanates from Jew to Gentile, will one day return to the Jew (Rom 11:28-36 cf. vs 11-12). Paul even indicates when this will happen: when the "fullness of the Gentiles has come in" (Rom 11:25). At that stage "all Israel shall be saved",[25] a reference to Isaiah 59:20. Interestingly, the very next verse in that Isaiah passage declares God's covenant with ethnic Israel is forever, while in Romans 11 Paul also goes on to explains how, in the context of Israel, the gifts and callings of God are irrevocable (Rom 11:29).

This theme of Israel abiding forever is echoed several times in the Bible. They include Jeremiah 31, well known for its reference to a new covenant in verses 31-34. But we hear considerably less about the verses which follow, where God declares that Israel will not cease to be a nation before Him (31:35-37). Are we to allegorise every reference to a perpetual Israel throughout human history? More importantly, if Isaiah was bringing a message of hope to a literal nation at an actual time, an esoteric allegorised message would have offered little by way of comfort to the original listeners and readers.[26]

---

[24] i.e. the opposite of particularism, rather than that theological concept of universalism which holds to the view that everyone shall be saved.

[25] Verse 26. See also Acts 13:23.

[26] Without doubt hermeneutics is crucial to this debate, with pro-Palestinian Evangelicals drawing strongly on an allegorical approach (for example, Chapman cites Philo of Alexandria during his discussion of the land, 142-3), and pro-Israel Christian Zionists favouring a strongly literal interpretation. Without due care and hermeneutical consistency such a reading of Scripture can become overly literal (for example, the New Jerusalem of Rev 21:2 means so much more than the restoration of the earthly city of Jerusalem), yet conversely supercessionists must take care

Eschatologically, too, the Bible has much to say about Israel. I am not talking about popular eschatology that seeks to marry prophecy with present world events. Such an approach is often speculative, even sensational, aimed more at selling books than anything else. But in reacting against such extremes, some Evangelicals go too far the other way, throwing out the eschatological baby with the dispensational bathwater. After all, Heilsgechichte (salvation history) covers the *whole* of human existence, and if the Church has no overriding eschatological hope to draw upon, what is the point? That is *not* to ignore other core themes brought about and concluded through Christ's work (whether, for example, redemptive or ecclesiological). Yet as we noted in Soulen's useful work at the beginning of this paper, the eschatological culmination of the age, including its personal and cosmic ramifications, and the promise of spending eternity with Christ are absolutely vital and central aspects of the Bible's metanarrative. Eschatology represents the conclusive outworking of salvation history, marking the stage when history ends and eternity begins. Thus the Gospels present the Kingdom of God as realised *and* eschatological, inaugurated but *not yet* fulfilled.[27] Even the famous liberal theologian Albert Schweitzer pointed out how Jesus' message was ultimately and thoroughly eschatological (even if Schweitzer himself believed Jesus was wrong).

The house of Israel features strongly in this eschatological scheme. In Romans 11:25-6 (cf Is 59:20-1) Paul declares all Israel shall be saved. That this event occurs 'after the fullness of the Gentiles has come in' indicates he has an eschatological event in mind. This juxtaposition of Israel's eschatological salvation, their

---

not simply to go the other way to defend an *a priori* view of what constitutes Israel in the New Testament.

[27] The debate among biblical scholars concerning the timing of the kingdom is well known. Passages which clearly portray the eschatological aspect of the Kingdom of God include Mt 13:47-50, 25:1 (during Jesus' eschatological discourse), Lk 22:16-18, Rev 11:15, 12:10.

washing and cleansing (of sin), and the giving of God's spirit to His chosen people is a theme taken up in Zechariah's eschatological discourse (12:10, 13:1 cf Ezekiel 18:31, 36:26-7, see also Isa 44:1-3, Jn 3:5).[28] Zechariah 12, a clearly eschatological passage, speaks of armies congregating upon Jerusalem and Israel for battle, echoing the final battle described in Revelation. The prophet Joel, too, describes such a battle and the very close linguistic similarities between Joel and Revelation 9 is not lost on Bible scholars. So either the author of Revelation merely copies Joel and reports a past prophecy *ex eventu*,[29] or else both are referring to a future event, a catastrophe to befall Israel. In fact, Joel takes a contemporary catastrophe (the plague of locusts which destroys the land) and projects it far into the eschatological future, detailing not only an invading army's invasion of Israel, but how through God's intervention Israel shall be saved physically and spiritually (thus bringing us full circle back to Romans 11:25-6). The central theme in Joel is the 'day of the Lord', a well known apocalyptic phrase cited five times in this short book. Yet again this event juxtaposes Israel's eschatological salvation, her cleansing from sin, and the pouring out of God's spirit upon her.

Granted, Peter draws on Joel 2 to explain the outpouring of God's spirit in Acts 2. But the apocalyptic scenario set out by Joel (wonders in the sky, blood, fire, smoke, darkness, moon likened to blood) is not present in the manner described in Revelation. As both books are eschatological, the outpouring is likely two-fold, or takes place in two stages: Pentecost and an end-times washing of

---

[28] The "heart of stone" detailed in Ezekiel is likely an allusion to the tablets of stone that contained the Law, symbols of the old covenant replaced with a new covenant with the house of Israel (cf Jer 31:31-37) at the time of her eschatological salvation. Another passage worth considering here, apparently in an eschatological context, is Zech 8:23.

[29] Literally, 'after the event', whereby a writer describes a prophetic event *after* it has taken place but maintaining it is *yet to come*. Those arguing for this device often do so because they deny the concept of predictive prophecy.

Israel's sin and regeneration through God's Spirit. Immediately before his reference to the outpouring of God's Spirit, Joel likens spiritual blessing to the Holy Land's two rainy seasons (the former and latter rain). If Pentecost is the first (an event, incidentally, where all participants and observers were Jews and proselytes to Judaism), God's eschatological salvation of Israel ("when they shall look upon him who they have pierced", Zechariah 12:10) must be the second.

Isaiah presents two visions of the Messiah: Suffering Servant and Conquering King. Jesus inaugurated the Kingdom in microcosm, but various Messianic passages in Isaiah indicate a literal kingdom established on earth. One of Jesus' titles is the King of Israel.[30] (It was even nailed to His cross.) That he will establish a literal, earthly kingdom is somewhat more inspiring than Him simply being king of our hearts. If we take Isaiah's Conquering King motif seriously, then Jesus' teaching of the eschatological inauguration of His Kingdom must surely have a literal, eschatological outworking, so that the Son of David takes His throne over the house of Israel and the world. It certainly explains better those eschatological passages concerning His reign from Jerusalem and the mountain of the Lord (eg Micah 4:1-4). It also demonstrates that while the land may not necessarily be an issue now, eschatologically-speaking it returns to centre stage.[31]

Lest one is uncomfortable with the notion of partial, two-fold, or multiple fulfilments of prophecy, the Bible is full of this

---

[30] Mt 2:2, 27:11, Jn 1:49, 12:13.
[31] Bearing in mind Paul's reference to the 'full number of the Gentiles' coming in, Lk 21:24 echoes a similar phrase in an eschatological context, at which time the land again takes centre stage and comes back under Jewish control. The question is, are we are in those last days now? If so, then the establishment of modern day Israel indeed looks very much part of the divine plan. But if the end times are not yet upon us, it is equally possible to hold to the view of the Jews as God's chosen people and their eschatological restoration, without having to state dogmatically the establishment of modern Israel is divinely ordained.

phenomenon, whether the sign of a maiden with child (Isa 7:14 cf Mt 1:23), God calling His son out of Egypt (Hos 11:1 cf Mt 2:15), or the abomination that makes desolate. This latter example again has an eschatological fulfilment. In intertestamental times Antiochus IV Epiphanes slaughtered a pig to Zeus in the Temple, leading to the Maccabean revolt. Later, Pompey and Titus also defiled the Temple. Yet Jesus also refers to it in an eschatological context.[32] Moreover, if one really desired to be controversial it might be claimed the Dome on the Rock is such an abomination. After all, on the very hill where Abraham prepared to sacrifice his son Isaac (and all the theology that goes with that), and where Jesus' ancestor David bought the Temple Mount from Ornan the Jebusite, stands a Dome within which is permanently inscribed, "The Sonship of Jesus and the Trinity are false", and "It is not fitting that God should beget or father a child".[33] Such statements put the Danish cartoon protests in a new context, yet of course the Christian way is to turn the other cheek, even when human nature demands retraction of language against our Saviour which we find deeply offensive.

Clearly, Jesus supercedes the old covenant, the New Testament shifts its focus away from the land (for now) to a worldwide community of Christian believers, while for the time being the Kingdom has been inaugurated in our hearts. But the salvation story does not end there. The eschatological culmination of the age is a biblical theology theme which is *widely* represented throughout both Testaments. Another is the house of Israel. Moreover, in the Bible so often both are presented as going hand in hand. Thus, Israel merits closer attention as a biblical theme,

---

[32] In fact, much like Joel, Jesus' great eschatological discourse in Matthew 24-5 takes a (near) contemporary event (the fall of Jerusalem in AD 70) and projects it into the eschatological future to describe a catastrophe to befall the Jewish people (Mt 24:16-20). It is immediately after these events that Jesus describes the glorious return of the Son of Man (24:29-31).

[33] Moshe Sharon, 'Islam on the Temple Mount' in *Biblical Archaeological Review* 32.4 (July-August 2006), 42, 45.

not least because Paul says we as a wild olive tree have been grafted into it. Given the strong representation of Israel as a biblical theme, this inevitably has some bearing on how we view the modern state Israel. After all, as noted earlier 'Israel' in the New Testament is nearly always used in an ethnic context.

That is not to say everyone descended of Israel is of the house of Israel (Ro 9:6-7). Israel is a *corporate* entity, and individuals cannot claim special status simply because they are Jews. Neither should we assume there is no need to share the Gospel with Jews. Quite the contrary. Paul's method was always to visit the synagogues and preach to the Jew first, and extreme Christian Zionist groups who refuse to do so ignore Acts of the Apostles and Paul's ministry. Neither can we say with certainty that the current state of Israel is necessarily fulfilled prophecy. The speed and manner of its inception, its survival against the odds, and other recent historical events may lead many Christians to reach such a conclusion (indeed, I am sympathetic to this view, though not dogmatically so). But unless one maintains categorically that we are indeed in the last days, biblically-speaking one cannot declare with certainty that modern Israel represents fulfilled prophecy. (Conversely, neither can supercessionists maintain the opposite view.) Biblically, one can only make a case for ethnic Israel's restoration and eschatological salvation, nothing more. As such, Christian Zionists should not regard their support for Israel as essential for God to fulfil biblical prophecy. He does not require our help to carry out His plans, as if the fulfilment of prophecy is somehow dependent on humans (though listening to several Christian Zionists one might be forgiven for thinking so).[34]

---

[34] A point discussed by Stephen Sizer in *Christian Zionism: Road-map to Armageddon?* (Leicester: IVP, 2004). It is unfortunate Sizer takes an unnecessarily polemical and sensational stance, as well as his tendency to parody pro-Israel believers as extreme Christian Zionists, as any useful point such as this he makes is lost on a wider audience which rejects both his pejorative language and lack of objectivity.

A PRACTICAL RESPONSE TO THE PRESENT CONFLICT

Having offered a biblical theology case for Israel, I want to conclude this chapter by offering briefly a practical Christian response to the current Israeli-Palestinian conflict and the realities on the ground. After all, this is a complex issue which raises many questions for Christians. For example, how do we reconcile our common Judeo-Christian history and values with the situation some Palestinian Christians find themselves in? Conversely, how do we respond to Palestinian liberation theology, given that some Palestinian Christians have come close to understanding (if not condoning) suicide bombings on the basis of Samson's last act in the temple of Dagon? Moreover, there is a prominent Muslim element in this conflict that demands a Christian response. These are just some of the pressing issues this conflict raises demanding a practical response from Christians.

First, in a conflict where every act, word, or nuance is seized upon, it is important to research the history of the conflict and learn the facts. The present conflict did not begin with the First or Second Intifadas, Yom Kippur (1973), or even the 1967 Six-Day War. In the wake of the Holocaust which nearly completely destroyed European Jewry, in 1947 the U.N. agreed a partition plan to create two nations, one Arab, the other Jewish. But we can go further back still, to the Arab-Jewish tensions of 1920s and 1930s British-controlled Palestine (largely fuelled by the Grand Mufti of Jerusalem, a sympathiser of Adolf Hitler),[35] or the British government's irreconcilable promises made to both the Jewish and Arab populations. In fact, we can go beyond the earliest Zionists in the late nineteenth century and note a sizeable and continuous Jewish presence in the Holy Land since biblical times.

Consider also the issue of land ownership. It is easy to reduce the conflict today to one of Israel stealing land. Indeed, the West Bank is presently under occupation (which many Israelis oppose),

---

[35] Martin Gilbert discusses at length the role the Grand Mufti in *Jerusalem in the Twentieth Century* (London: Pimlico, 1996).

but much of the land within Israel's internationally-recognised borders was actually purchased in the early 1900s, sometimes for highly inflated prices.[36] Today Haredi Jews are buying up Arab homes on the Ophel Ridge (the original City of David south of the Temple Mount and overlooking the Kidron Valley) at above-market prices to secure a Jewish presence on a ridge of major historical, political, and religious significance for Jews. Conversely, the Jordanian government is buying up as much land and property as possible to retain its influence in the sensitive Temple Mount vicinity.[37] Thus, beyond the emotive language and propaganda not everything is as it seems. There are realities on the ground that must be understood before we engage in any theological treatment of the conflict, and Christians do well not to rush to judgment or speak hastily without having moved beyond the rhetoric and ascertained the facts (Prov 29:20, Jas 1:19-20).

Consider, for example, Ariel Sharon's plan for withdrawal from Gaza. In light of the intensification of rocket attacks from a recently-unoccupied Gaza on Israeli towns such as Sderot, together with the Palestinian civil war and Hamas' seizure of Gaza, Sharon's withdrawal plan was clearly a strategic miscalculation. Also, by returning land for peace Israel has rarely reaped a peace dividend (the return of Sinai to Egypt being a notable exception), with extremism intensifying in Southern Lebanon and Gaza. Yet leaving these political realities aside, the fact remains that in biblical times present-day Gaza covered, in large part, the territory of the Philistines (from where the word `Palestine' originates). Nonetheless, Christian Zionists

---

[36] For example, see Martin Gilbert, *The Routledge Atlas of the Arab-Israeli Conflict* (London: Routledge, 2002), 12. Colin Chapman also discusses in some detail how early Zionists purchased land from absentee Arab landlords (*Whose Promised Land?* 59-61).

[37] Aaron Klein, `Jordan secretly buying land accessing Temple Mount', *World Net Daily* (3 July 2007).
www.worldnetdaily.com/news/article.asp?ARTICLE_ID=56483 (last accessed 14 July 2007).

vociferously excoriated Ariel Sharon for his Gaza withdrawal precisely on theological grounds. Moreover, as noted earlier, land is but one dimension of nationhood, and just as biblical Israel existed in Babylonian exile, or Persian, Greek, and Roman occupation, so today giving up some land for peace does not dilute Israel's nationhood (though from a theological perspective it is God's to give and take away, not Israel's), even if the present volatile climate makes it politically unrealistic. The fact is, there are realities on the ground that simply cannot be ignored by either side. Israel has no intention of modifying its harsh stance as long as it faces a very real security threat. Neither are the Palestinians going to go away or renounce their claims to statehood. When responding to this issue, pro-Israel and pro-Palestinian Christians have no choice but to confront these realities.

Second, if the Bible prohibits false witness, demands justice, and even highlights the importance of measuring with properly calibrated scales (Lev 19:36, Am 8:5, Mic 6:11), then surely even-handedness is an essential biblical principle when exploring this conflict. Thus, our treatment of *all* the issues must be fair and balanced. For example, though Palestine was a desolate backwater when the first Zionists arrived in the 1880s and 1890s, nonetheless the fact remains it was not an empty land. Though immigration statistics in this regard are notoriously sketchy and unreliable, there is an argument to be made concerning how Zionist economic success encouraged not only an influx of Jews to Palestine in the early twentieth century, but also Arab immigrants from other parts of the Arab world. But once again, the fact remains that the land was not empty when the first Zionists emigrated to the Holy Land, and as both populations grew it was inevitable that one would be pushed to one side.

Neither can we justify an "Israel right or wrong" mentality, as some Christians seek to do. Israel sinned even in biblical times, so to ignore her present injustices and sinful behaviour is wrong. There seems little doubt that a gung-ho Israeli military doctrine (which owes something to U.S. military doctrine and methods) has often resulted in what is euphemistically termed `collateral damage'. It is one thing to highlight Israeli actions over security concerns, but quite another to ignore her errors of judgement (or the activities of some `bad apples' within the army, much like troops anywhere else), though we should also differentiate between deliberate harshness and the inevitable *Realpolitik* Israel practices (which a liberal West no longer has the stomach for). It should be noted that Israeli ruthlessness is born out of very real security needs.

Conversely, Israel has faced an existential threat since her inception. Even within hours of declaring statehood she was attacked by various neighbouring Arab nations. Iran's Mahmoud Ahmadinejad openly and frequently calls for Israel's annihilation, as do Hamas and Hizbollah. Yet too often, many people (including some pro-Palestinian Christians) insist on exacting a higher standard from Israel than, for example, China, Zimbabwe, the architects of Darfur, and some of the authoritarian Arab nations. After all, Israel is a democratic country which extends more rights to its Arab Israeli citizens than some autocratic Arab countries. Meanwhile many Palestinians are frustrated with their leaders and simply want to get on with their lives.[38] Thus, we do well as Christians to explore this issue objectively and even-handedly, getting beyond the rhetoric to uncover and consider the underlying facts on both sides.

This leads to a third point: Christians should set their *own* agenda for the treatment of this issue, rather than be influenced by the political left, U.S. foreign policy, or propaganda from one side or the other. Listening to some of them, one could be forgiven for

---

[38] Several years ago an Arab Jerusalemite taxi driver I chatted with brought up the issue of Israeli Prime Minister Ehud Barak's substantial peace offer. He was at a loss to understand why Yasser Arafat had turned it down, going on to express resentment against Palestinian leaders for not making peace with the Israelis so that everyone in the region could get on with improving their lives and economic wellbeing. I have heard such sentiment echoed several times among everyday Palestinians.

almost believing that many Christian Zionists sit in the Knesset, while some pro-Palestinian Christians appear as apologists for Arab nationalism, and even Islam. A minority of Palestinian Christians, too, have arguably been influenced by the Palestinian political agenda, rather than a Christian worldview. Why else do they vocally denounce Israel and highlight their own plight, yet rarely speak out against wholesale massacres of Christians in parts of Indonesia, Pakistan, or other Muslim nations? Or why is Palestinian Muslim economic targeting of Christian business, together with physical abuse of Christians in the Palestinian territories by Muslim extremists, ignored?[39] That many Palestinian Christians refuse to embrace liberation theology agenda and denounce Israel, choosing instead to turn the other cheek in the face of Muslim persecution or at-times Israeli heavy-handedness indicates that these Christians, at least, have not permitted outsiders to influence or dictate the agenda.

The psalmist instructs his audience to pray for the peace of Jerusalem (Ps 122:6), while Jesus expressed great love and tenderness for the house of Israel, even likening His love for Jerusalem to a hen gathering her chicks under her wings.[40] Conversely, Psalm 83:3-4 states:

> *They lay crafty plans against your people; they consult together against your treasured ones. They say, "Come, let us wipe them out as a nation; let the name of Israel be remembered no more!"*

---

[39] For a discussion, see Daniel Pipes, 'Disappearing Christians in the Middle East', *Middle East Quarterly* (Winter 2001). The entire issue of this journal, which is devoted to Christianity in the Middle East, is available online at www.meforum.org/meq/issues/200101. See also Elizabeth Day, 'O Muslim Town of Bethlehem', *Daily Mail*, 16 December 2006, and Tim Butcher, 'Why Bethlehem's Christians Are Still Voting With Their Feet', *Daily Telegraph*, 20 December 2006.
[40] Mt 23:37, Lk 13:34.

As in the psalmist's day, Israel today faces an existential threat by enemies who regard her annihilation a religious duty. And unlike the Western mindset, so driven by hedonism and instant gratification, these enemies have a much more long-term outlook and goal. In 2006 I listened to a Hamas spokesman liken the current conflict to the Crusades, declaring that although it took over a century to remove the Crusaders, they succeeded in time, just as they would with the annihilation of Israel one day.

Christians clearly must pray for fellow believers living in the Holy Land, so that through their actions and witness both Jews and Arabs might know Christ. Not only that, but if indeed the house of Israel still retains a special place in God's heart and plans, and as the Middle East conflict shifts from a purely political to a religio-political Islamist conflict that threatens Israel's very existence, then surely Christians must pray for Israel also.

CHAPTER 3

Apostolic Jewish-Christian Hermeneutics and Supercessionism[1]

Jacob Prasch

Many people looking at the issue of replacement theology tend do so from an historical, theological or ethnic perspective. Fewer explore the issue from a hermeneutical angle. In this chapter, then, my aim is to explore how, throughout its history, the church has often failed to employ the methods of biblical interpretation practised by the Apostles and a Jewish first century church. This survey offers two observations relating to the wider issue of supercessionism, one directly, the other indirectly. First, a shift away from how the first century church interpreted the Scriptures has given rise to a form of allegorical, or symbolic interpretation of the Bible which has contributed to the rise of supercessionism. Meanwhile, this supercessionism has resulted in much of the church ditching a Jewish interpretation of Scripture, resulting in it missing out considerably in its interpretation and application of the Bible.

TWO HERMENEUTICAL SCHOOLS

During the Patristic period[2] two separate schools of hermeneutics emerged, one associated with the city of Antioch in the Middle East, the other with Alexandria, in what is now Egypt. Both

---

[1] The following chapter is based on a conference paper and several lectures delivered by Jacob Prasch at the Midlands Bible College (now King's Evangelical Divinity School). The material has been conflated, edited and adapted for use here by the volume editor with the permission of the speaker.

[2] From the second to eighth centuries.

schools would eventually come to dominate how the church, at different times during much of its history, interpreted the Bible.

The Antiochene school, generally followed by the Eastern Church Fathers, emphasised a literal approach to the interpretation of the Bible. The Alexandrian school, on the other hand, took a more symbolic approach in how it interpreted Scripture. This allegorical hermeneutic (a mystical approach which moves beyond the plain, literal meaning to seek a hidden, deeper meaning and base doctrines on it) already existed within Judaism, as expressed by Philo, a Jew who lived in Alexandria. I believe neither school offered a hermeneutical methodology faithful to that practised by the Apostles and the New Testament church. However, the Antiochene school strayed away less from Scripture than its Alexandrian counterpart because, being more literal in its interpretation of the Bible, it was less prone to error.

Eventually, the Alexandrian school became the dominant hermeneutical approach to the Bible during the medieval church period. This was because after the Emperor Constantine pseudo-Christianised the Roman Empire in the fourth century, the theologian Augustine of Hippo (AD 354-430) redefined Christianity by drawing on the thought of the Greek philosopher Plato. Platonic thought, which was the dominant worldview at the time, fitted in nicely with the Alexandrian school's emphasis on the allegorical interpretation of the Bible so favoured by the likes of Philo, Clement and Origen. It is important to note that, to this day, replacement theology draws upon this Alexandrian approach, allegorising and spiritualising passages in the Bible relating to Israel and instead appropriating them as promises for the church.

The Alexandrian allegorical approach suited the purposes of medieval Roman Catholicism, especially the papal office, very well. Its emphasis on a mystical, subjective interpretation of Scripture and a *sensus plenior* (deeper meaning from God) went hand in hand with the view biblical interpretation was the privy domain of a pope who claimed to be the direct heir of the Apostle Peter (who Catholics regard as the very first pope). It allowed the pope to speak as if from the chair of Peter himself (known as *ex cathedra*). In other words, when the pope makes a theological declaration it is regarded as infallible. (Actually, I can show you plenty of popes who contradicted other popes, but of course they do not like to discuss that too much.)

Thus, for hundreds of years, stretching from the end of the Patristic era to the Reformation, the dominant intellectual and hermeneutical approach to the Bible was based on medieval scholasticism and heavily influenced by the Alexandrian school. It resulted in a form of hermeneutics which drew heavily on symbolism, and indeed made symbolism and type the basis for *new* doctrine, rather than the correct approach, which is to utilise symbolism and typology to illustrate *existing* doctrines. The result was a form of medieval Gnosticism (Gnosticism was an early church heresy stating salvation came through secret knowledge imparted to a chosen few), whereby a medieval church taught doctrines on the basis of secret knowledge, or allegorical interpretation, which was the private realm of the pope and Catholic elites. I have seen this same hermeneutic, which emphasises special, esoteric insight by the leadership, among hyper-Pentecostals and my fellow Charismatics, most notably the Kansas City Prophets, who do something very similar. They take a passage out of context, spiritualising and imbuing it with a subjective, mystical meaning to suit their own purposes, thus creating a pretext.

In the sixteenth century the Reformers rejected this approach to the Bible, ditching allegorical interpretation and instead taking a strongly literalist line, much like John Calvin's commentary of a piece of secular literature, Seneca's *De Clementia*. Thus, with the Reformation we see an important historical shift within the church, from an Alexandrian to a much more Antiochene approach, focusing on the plain, literal meaning of Scripture. This Western Protestant focus on the plain meaning, history and language of the Bible text is known as *grammatico-historical interpretation*.

Western grammatico-historical interpretation is all well and good, but from the perspective of first century Jewish Christianity I contend it is right in what it confirms yet wrong in what it omits. It allows people to see the basic truth and as such pointed people back to the Gospel. The grammatico-historical approach focused on many important things, such text, context, induction above deduction, exegesis above eisegesis, and so on, and the essentials of this approach are correct. But it did not travel far enough down the road towards restoring a first century Jewish Christian hermeneutic. Let me put it this way: if you work in a corner shop, you only need arithmetic; but if you want to be a rocket scientist, you need calculus. Both arithmetic and calculus are mathematics, but the latter takes the discipline of mathematics much further. Likewise, if you want to understand, say, properly apocalyptic literature in the Bible, you cannot limit a study of it to the grammatico-historical approach. Quite simply, you will never fully understand Jewish apocalyptic literature if you only interpret it with the linguistic and historical tools of grammatico-historical interpretation. Something more is needed, which some people began to realise some time after the Reformation.

RENEWED INTEREST IN JEWISH HERMENEUTICS

There have been efforts stretching back for some four hundred years to restore a Jewish understanding of biblical interpretation. The first major figure to attempt this was an Englishman, a Puritan by the name of John Lightfoot, who wrote a midrashic commentary during the time of Cromwell. Another Puritan, John Robinson, a chaplain to the Puritan Fathers who sailed on the *Mayflower* to the North America, was of the opinion that, "there is more light in God's Word than we presently see". He understood there were things the Apostles knew concerning the Scriptures which the church had lost sight of. Such Puritans believed the

Reformation's emphasis on *Sola Scriptura*[3] was important, that it had helped put the church back on the right track to appropriating correct biblical interpretation. But what was needed was to continue travelling *further* down that track. The Puritans and several others recognised, for the most part, this had not happened in any significant way.

It was not until the nineteenth century, with the emergence of the early Dispensationalists and the Plymouth Brethren, that a New Testament Jewish-Christian hermeneutic took a closer step. These people began to take a perspective of Scripture that closely resembles what I would call *midrash,* which was arguably how the New Testament church viewed Scripture and handled typology. (The term and concept of midrash is introduced to us in 2 Chronicles 13:22, where it translated "treatise". Although Kings and Chronicles are largely synoptic in their structural delimitation of narratives, the Books of Kings emphasise the account of a royal reign from a *biographical* perspective, while the Books of Chronicles places more emphasis on the *historical* perspective. In the parallel biographical account of Abijah in Kings we are synoptically informed of the historical deeds of Abijah in Chronicles, yet Chronicles informs us the deeds are further recorded midrashically by an obscure figure known to us as Iddo.) This was probably the closest the Gentile church has come to interpreting correctly the Scriptures as a Jewish book, like the Apostles did. Sadly, the Plymouth Brethren, once a dynamic movement, largely disintegrated over time, which is a tragedy for a variety of reasons, not least their many virtues.

Aside from these church efforts, there were also several scholarly (particularly German) attempts to engage in a Jewish interpretation of the New Testament. Yet such efforts soon became bogged down in academic debate. More recently,

---

[3] Literally 'Scripture only', a Reformation emphasis upon the Bible as the final authority on all issues of Christian belief and practice, rather than other authorities, for example, the church or papal decree, which the Reformers reacted against.

however, the Jewish scholar Jacob Neusner has argued the New Testament represents an important, even pivotal, body of Second Temple period Jewish literature located between the inter-testamental Jewish writings and the post-New Testament rabbinic writings. Many rabbis dismiss the New Testament as a Gentile distortion of the Jewish Scriptures, but when major academic figures such as Neusner and others argue the New Testament is thoroughly Jewish in its literary forms and genre, this is a powerful apologetic in Jewish evangelism. Importantly, it should be noted such scholars do not believe in Jesus, they simply seek to explore the New Testament from the perspective of Jewish scholarship. Nonetheless, they reach the conclusion that the New Testament is, to all intents and purposes, thoroughly Jewish. Not only does this directly contradict Protestant liberal views that the New Testament narratives (particularly in the gospels) are fabrications by a later Gentile church, more importantly, it highlights how major Jewish scholars increasingly recognise the thoroughly Jewish nature of the New Testament. In short, the New Testament church is a Jewish church, which in turn has led to increasing academic interest in the Jewish roots of Christianity. Significantly, some of these studies also identify a New Testament hermeneutic reflecting the culture of first century Palestinian Judaism, but which much of the church today has lost.

EARLY RABBINIC HEREMENEUTICS AND THE NEW TESTAMENT

In recent years, with the discovery and study of the Dead Sea Scrolls at Qumran, scholars have noted the manner in which the New Testament handles and interprets the Old Testament, which parallels how the Dead Sea Scrolls handle the Old Testament. When we consider this New Testament use of the Old, it is noticeably quite different to how much of the Western Church traditionally interprets the Bible. (Incidentally, I believe one of the gravest threats to the church today is how many leaders do not follow an apostolic model of ecclesiology, increasingly drawing on a medieval church model and emphasising things such as contemplative prayer, regarded as the means to restore the Christian ideal. Instead of going back to the book of Acts and the New Testament, they draw on the monasticism and mysticism of the Dark Ages.) Liberal Protestant scholars, particularly people like Rudolf Bultmann in the early twentieth century, focused on what we call the *Sitz im Leben*, or life setting and context, of the Bible text. But their approach (known as form criticism) assumed most of the narratives in the gospels were the invention (or embellishment) of a *later*, less Jewish church. For the form critics, then, a focus on Sitz im Leben was an attempt to get back to the life setting of what they assumed was a New Testament text written by a late first and early second century, predominantly Gentile church, rather than the Sitz im Leben of the early apostolic (and thus Jewish) church described in the Bible.

But recent studies of the Dead Sea Scrolls demonstrate how the New Testament is *not* an invention of a later Gentile church. Rather, its literary style, together with the manner in which the New Testament authors handled the Old Testament is *thoroughly* Jewish. Thus, a *peshat-pesher* approach (which we will look at shortly) eventually forced J.A.T. Robinson, the noted liberal scholar, to reverse his position on the dating of the Gospels, acknowledging they had to be the product of a much earlier Jewish church, rather than a fabrication or embellishment by a later Gentile church.

So it is essential we take into account the Sitz im Leben of the text and when it was written – not the setting postulated by the form critics, but the thoroughly Jewish milieu in which the New Testament was written, as demonstrated by the Dead Sea Scrolls. So when we focus on the Sitz im Leben of the New Testament writings, we are focusing on how they are culturally, literally and theologically the product of early first century Jewish society. Also, and very importantly, we must not focus just on the cultural setting of the text, but also how the authors' historical, cultural and theological backgrounds led them to interpret Scripture. Consider how, for example, Paul was a disciple of Rabbi Gamaliel, the grandson of Hillel. There were two major Pharisee schools, and Hillel represented one of them, and this theological and hermeneutical background inevitably had a bearing on how Paul and handled Scripture. Therefore, you simply cannot divorce biblical interpretation from the Jewish Sitz im Leben in which the New Testament was written.

So how did rabbis in the first century church interpret Scripture? The essential principles of midrashic hermeneutics which helped to frame the hermeneutics of the Apostolic church are the Seven Middoth of Rabbi Hillel, from the rabbinic academy where Rabbi Shaul of Tarsus (Paul The Apostle) was schooled by Gamaliel. The two most important of these are *Qal wahomer* (light to heavy; general truths become amplified in importance in weighty situations) and *Binyan 'ab mishene kethubim* (building a doctrinal argument from two texts; where cognate circumstances, idioms and metaphors occur the texts referentially relate and the same exegetical considerations must apply to both). Rabbis also employed what we refer to as the *mashal-nimshal* format. A *mashal* is a description of something from everyday life (for example, something from nature), while *nimshal* is its spiritual interpretation or application. Let me illustrate it thus:

Like a gold ring in a pig's snout [mashal]
is a beautiful woman without discretion. [nimshal]
(Prov 11:22)

A word fitly spoken [nimshal]
is like apples of gold in a setting of silver. [mashal]
(Prov 25:11)

We can employ this approach in our interpretation of the parables. Western hermeneutics has sought to understand parables in terms of correspondence: high correspondence - low correspondence. But a first century Jew would not have approached parable the way a Western scholar would. Instead, they would have explored parable from the point of view of *mashal-nimshal*. Indeed, the parables are simply elongated mashals. A *mashal is* a proverb – in fact, in Hebrew the book of Proverbs is called *Mishle (Shlomoh)*, the Proverbs (of Solomon), or the book of *mashals.* To the Jewish mind in biblical days, a parable would simply have been regarded as an elongated *mashal*, expressed in the form of a story. This was central to their understanding and interpretation.

This would have been particularly relevant to Jesus' listenership when He spoke the parables. In first century Jewish society, although people were literate, the *Am ha'Aretz* (common people, lit. 'the people of the land') would learn things by rote, that is, through stories. So by teaching in parables Jesus was appealing to the *Am ha'Aretz*. He would take theological concepts and make them comprehensible and practical for ordinary people. Other rabbis also used parables, but unlike Jesus they would not explain or interpret this to people. Consider Jesus' interpretation of the parable of the vineyard, in which the owner's servants and son were killed by the workers. The Pharisees knew He spoke it about them (Matt 21:45), in other words, they were able to interpret the parable, but they kept silent. Interpretation, or knowledge, was for the initiated only, and so they refused to teach it to the everyday folk. You see, knowledge is power, but the Pharisees kept their knowledge to themselves to help retain their position as not only a theological, but also a social, economic and political elite. In Luke 11:52 we read how the scribes sought to retain the keys of knowledge. So when Jesus came preaching and teaching, He was, in effect, taking away from the Jewish religious teachers the hermeneutical keys and giving them to the Apostles, the poor people He preached to, and even (eventually) the Gentiles. Imagine how this upset the applecart!

Another feature of rabbinic interpretation is *peshat* and *pesher.* Peshat is the simple, straightforward meaning, while pesher is what it actually means theologically or spiritually. A Western interpretation of John's gospel would differ considerably from that of a first century Jew. Consider, for example, the similarities between the Creation account in Genesis (peshat) and the book of John, which the evangelist[4] presents as a new creation (pesher). At Creation God walks the earth and Adam hears Him walking in the garden, while in John's gospel God walks the earth in the new creation. In Genesis, God separates the light from dark, while in John God likewise comes to separate light from darkness. In the Creation narrative you have the small light and the great light, while in John's new creation you have Jesus (the greater light) and John the Baptist (the lesser light). In Genesis the Spirit moves on the water and brings forth the creation, while in John 3:5, when Jesus talks of being born of the water and spirit, the Spirit moves on the water and brings forth a new creation. In the Creation narrative, on the third day, God does a miracle with water; and so in the new creation narrative in John, on the third day of the wedding of Canaan, God does a miracle with water. God begins his first plan for mankind with a nuptial, a wedding, between Adam and Eve. In John, God begins His second plan for mankind with a nuptial, when Jesus launches His ministry at the wedding at Canaan.   In Genesis there is the tree of life. Ancient sources inform us that in Judaism the fig tree represents the Tree of Life. Now when Jesus tells Nathanael, "I saw you under the fig tree" (John 1:48), what did He mean? A strictly literal interpretation would not see anything significant about this event, but there is more to this narrative than the literal meaning. Jesus indeed saw Nathanael under a literal fig tree, but what He was saying to Nathanael in Hebrew metaphor was this: "I saw you from the Garden, the creation, from the foundation of the World. I saw you under the fig tree, the Tree of Life, right at the beginning." Now all this makes perfect sense to a Jewish Christian in the first century, or to a Messianic Jew, but it has lost this sense to much of the Western Church. Instead of taking a hermeneutical approach from the Apostles, they draw on an approach from the sixteenth century.

---

[4] The technical term for an author of one of the four gospels.

Another example can be found in Hosea 11:1 which states, "When Israel was a child, I loved him, and out of Egypt I called my son." Note how Hosea makes a retroactive reference back to the Exodus under Moses. Yet Matthew (2:15) takes the same quote from Hosea and, in the context of Jesus' nativity, he says this is about *Jesus* coming out of Egypt. According to liberal Western exegesis and its focus on history, Matthew takes the text completely out of context in an unscientific way. But actually, within a first century Jewish understanding this is a classic case of the *peshat-pesher* approach. The Exodus (peshat) points to Jesus (pesher). Jewish hermeneutics would have followed a motif, in this case the Exodus event. But this motif begins, not with Jesus or the Exodus itself, but rather with Abraham. During a famine Abraham goes to Egypt, God judges Pharaoh, and Abraham *comes out* of Egypt. Abraham's biological descendants, the children of Israel, also go to Egypt during a famine. Likewise, they *come out* under Moses, and again God judges a wicked king, Pharaoh. It happens to Abraham, the father of all who believe, and so it also happens to the nation of Israel, his descendants. Likewise, Jesus fits the same pattern: God judges Herod, another wicked king, and the Messiah comes out of Egypt. Moreover, in his discussion in 1 Corinthians 10, when we are saved, Paul says, metaphorically *we also* come out of Egypt (Egypt being a picture of the world, while Pharaoh is a picture of Satan, the god of the world). Thus the Exodus motif continues. As Moses made covenant with blood, sprinkled it and took the people of Israel out of Egypt through the water into the Promised Land, so Jesus covers us with the blood of the Paschal Lamb and takes us through baptism into heaven. At salvation we – the church – are also called out of Egypt. Also, in the Passion narratives we see a typological recycling of Paschal themes using a peshet–pesher format, the Exodus providing the peshat and the execution of the Messiah furnishing the pesher.

But it does not end there; there is also a future exodus. In a Passover *seder* there is the commemoration of the judgments of Egypt to this day: darkness, blood, frogs, the cup of God's wrath filling up. And these same judgements on Egypt are replayed eschatologically in the book of Revelation. Moreover, the manner in which Pharaoh's magicians counterfeited the miracles of Moses and Aaron is a picture, a type, of the way the Antichrist and false prophets will counterfeit the miracles of Jesus and His witnesses (Matt 24:24). Also, why did they bring Joseph's bones out of Egypt? The dead in Christ rise first. It is a picture of the *parousia* (the second coming), in other words, it is a motif (the same motif, that of Exodus). So as we have noted, the Exodus motif can be applied to Abraham or Israel, but it equally applies to Jesus. Paul also takes the same Exodus motif and applies it to the church in 1 Corinthians 10, while Revelation takes the same motif, the Exodus story, and applies it to the rapture and resurrection. This is quite different from the way some in the Western Church relying solely on sixteenth century hermeneutics might understand Hosea 11:1 and Matthew's use of this text.

Having mentioned the end times, it is worth at this stage dwelling a little further on a Jewish understanding of eschatology. The intertestamental period saw the development of a preoccupation with the end times (*eschaton*) and the messianic age, which much of the church today has lost. Moreover, Western theologians tend to insist on the need to hold to one of four main approaches to the study of the end times. Consider how a typical Western college or seminary will detail four main approaches to end-time prophesy: preterism, historicism, idealism (symbolism) and futurism. Preterism says it has already happened (in grammar, the preterite tense is a verb in the past tense). So it is argued the events described in Revelation occurred in the first century at the time of the Fall of Jerusalem in AD 70. So there is no Antichrist, no falling away, or Great Tribulation. All this happened in the first century, it is maintained. Historicism, on the other hand, is the view the Reformers favoured, which focuses on an *ongoing* historical dynamic featuring the pope and Roman Catholicism. Thus, historicists regard the Antichrist as an institution, rather than a person. Meanwhile, idealists (symbolists) see Revelation as holding symbolic truths and ideals, rather than a description of actual historical events, whether in the past or present. Revelation, then, is regarded more or less as poetry, designed to encourage us in times of persecution and hardship and to assure us during these periods that the Lord is coming. Then there is futurism, associated with the series by Tim LeHaye. This is the view that everything (or nearly everything) described in Revelation is yet to happen.

So a Western mindset expects you to choose one of these eschatological positions. However, the Jewish approach says it is not a case of choosing *any one*, but rather *all four*. Consider how in Matthew 24 Jesus spoke eschatologically of the abomination of desolation spoken of by Daniel, something that had already happened. So the abomination of desolation is presented by Jesus as both in the past *and* the future, preterist and futurist. Meanwhile, we see various examples or types of the abomination of desolation throughout history, whether that prophesied by Daniel (fulfilled under Antiochus IV Epiphanes), Pompey's desecration of the Temple before Jesus was born, Titus's destruction of Jerusalem in AD 70, Julian the Apostate's attempt to rebuild the temple, or what Jesus prophesied about in the eschatological future in Matthew 24. Meanwhile, at this time on the Temple Mount is the Dome of the Rock, which has an inscription stating God has no son. However, 1 John 2:22 states he who denies the Father-Son relationship is Antichrist. So from a Christian perspective the inscription in the Dome is an affront, an abomination to the very central revelation of Christianity, that Jesus is the Son of God. Thus in all these cases, just as in historicism, we see an historical, repeated expression of the Antichrist. Meanwhile, the events described in Revelation also draw on catastrophic events which occurred in the first century, at a time when the church desperately needed encouragement. And so we see an idealist, symbolic comfort for suffering Christians. So in the Western mind, you tend to hold to any one of these four eschatological positions. But actually, the truth is to be found in *all four,* and the Jewish approach is not to be forced into making an artificial choice like this.

Akin to apocalyptic, midrash relates both to the hermeneutical method and literary genre (type of literature) bearing the name. Just as we have apocalyptic material defined from a literary perspective, requiring hermeneutical considerations appropriate to symbolic entities, numbers, typologies, and metaphors for conflict with anti-heroes and protagonists in portions of Ezekiel, Isaiah, Joel, Daniel and Zechariah, so in the New Testament we have a book composed in the genre bearing the name – the Book of Revelation – which is a treatise drawing on Old Testament apocalyptic themes. Likewise, the epistle of Jude is a midrashic treatise. It employs pesher interpretations of Old Testament motifs, applying them to the circumstances being addressed in the early church.

Midrashic pesher is nowhere more indispensible than in eschatology. New Testament eschatology essentially borrows the themes of the final days of pre-Exilic Samaria in 721 BC and the final days of pre-exilic Judah in 586 BC from the books of Isaiah, Joel, Micah, Daniel, Jeremiah, and Ezekiel, as well as the events of 70 AD, and applies them all with midrashic pesher to the eschatological church. These themes include 'Fallen is Babylon', the destruction of the temple, and the pandemonium and confusion generated by a proliferation of false prophets among backslidden Israelites. New Testament eschatology, then, applies a pesher interpretation to future prophetic events, reinterpreting them as a future repetition of past events which are recorded in biblical history. Hence, efforts to explain New Testament eschatology by solely conventional grammatical-historical interpretation are implausible and have led to a reduction of a three-dimensional portrait of prophetic events to a two-dimensional portrait among those conservative Evangelicals favouring a sixteenth century exegetical approach, and to a one-dimensional reduction by the liberal proponents of higher critical presupposition. Yet when observed midrashically, New Testament eschatology fits the hermeneutics of Qumran eschatology like a glove. Thus, hermeneutics should not be extricated from Sitz im Leben.

CONCLUDING THOUGHTS

Within biblical hermeneutics we have noted two errors. There are those who base their doctrine on a symbolic or spiritual interpretation, and as such follow the Alexandrian school of interpretation. This is, hermeneutically at least, where supercessionism originates and finds sustenance, by allegorising promises for Israel in the Bible and spiritualising them for the church. Yet in the Jewish hermeneutics of the first century, the hermeneutics used by Jesus and Paul, you *never* base a doctrine on a type or a shadow.   Instead, you use a type or a shadow to illustrate doctrine or to illuminate it. For instance, we could set a Passover *seder* table and, comparing it with the last supper, illustrate the doctrine of atonement and substitutionary propitiation through the typology and the symbolism of the meal. But we do not base the doctrine on the symbolism, rather we use the symbolism to illuminate the doctrine. In Gnosticism it is the complete opposite: you base the doctrine on some kind of a symbolic meaning; you essentially negate the literal meaning in favour of a spiritual one. However, in *midrash* you *amplify* the literal meaning in light of the spiritual meaning. You *never* negate the literal, which is how the Jewish approach differs from allegorical interpretation. Neither do you ever base a doctrine on a type, or allegory, or hyperbole. This is deadly and it is dangerous. You use them to illustrate a doctrine. So *pesher* must not be confused, then, with Gnosticism. Ironically, at about the same time Christian hermeneutics deviated from a New Testament hermeneutical approach in the Patristic period, so too Rabbinic Judaism deviated away from this approach, resulting in a much more allegorical approach.

Then there are those who follow rigidly a strict grammatico-historical interpretation, focusing solely on the literal meaning. They state, "When the plain sense of Scripture makes sense, seek no further sense", or "There are many applications of a Scripture, but only one interpretation". But who says it has to be this way? Rabbis said there are multiple interpretations. With whom did Jesus agree? Consider, Jesus said "No sign will be given to this generation accept the sign of the prophet Jonah". Yet consider this statement synoptically. In one place the sign of the prophet Jonah is three days and three nights, in another place, it is Nineveh, where the Gentiles repented, contrasted with the Jews who refused to do so when Jesus preached. Thus, Jesus gives two entirely different interpretations for the sign of Jonah. In short, they are not mutually exclusive, they are simultaneously true. If I were to take a literal, Western approach, there would be only one interpretation. But Jesus Christ happens to disagree. He taught the way the rabbis did. By ditching Israel, we ditch the Jewish root of the church. As a negative bi-product of ditching the root, we miss out considerably on how a first century Jewish hermeneutic enhances our understanding of the Scriptures.

Further Reading
For an understanding of the Sitz im Leben of Judaism in the first century, consider E.P. Sanders' *Paul and Palestinian Judaism,* and also *Jesus and Judaism.* Alfred Edersheim's *Life and Times of Jesus the Messiah* is a nineteenth century but nonetheless provides useful insight into the cultural and religious world of first century Jews. Notable also is James H. Charlesworth, an Evangelical within the Ivy League, who notes a strong Jewish element within New Testament interpretation. Walter Kaiser's *Uses of the Old Testament in the New* offers a detailed treatment of the subject. For a very useful book exploring the Jewish nature of New Testament interpretation, see Richard Longenecker's *Biblical Exegesis in the Apostolic Period.* Finally, two books exploring the Jewish roots of the church are Marvin Wilson's *Our Father Abraham: Jewish Roots of the Christian Faith,* and Daniel Grubers' *The Church and the Jews: The Biblical Relationship.*

CHAPTER 4

A Calvinist Considers Israel's Right to the Land

Stephen M. Vantassel

To those familiar with Calvinist theology, it may seem unusual to be reading a defence of Israel's right to the land from that theological tradition. Historically Calvinism, and its umbrella view known as Covenant[1] or Reformed theology[2], has been allied with amillennial[3] and postmillennial views of eschatology. Reformed theology contends that Israel, as a distinct covenantal community, has been subsumed in and superseded by the Church. Since the Church, which lacks both ethnic and territorial claims, has replaced Israel (Gal 6:16), Israel has lost any continued right to the land.

So how can someone from a Calvinist perspective defend Israel's right to the land given that such a position has been traditionally the domain of premillennialists and Dispensationalists? Perhaps the answer lies in my relative newness to Calvinism. I was raised in an Arminian, Dispensational, and pre-millennial espousing household. I adopted Calvinism after

---

[1] Paul Enns, *The Moody Handbook of Theology* (Chicago: Moody Press, 1989), 503, 510.
[2] For the purposes of this paper, I am treating Covenantalists and Reformed theologians as synonymous.
[3] A-millennialism believes we are presently in the millennium. The thousand years is a figurative number. At the end of the Millennium there will be an outbreak of evil and an anti-Christ which will be followed by Christ's return to establish his final and perfect rule. www.reformedreader.org/mchart.htm Post-Millennialism of which a-millennialism is a subset, believes that the church will grow in influence until it establishes Christ's rule over the world. It is an optimistic eschatology. At the end, Armageddon will occur followed by Christ's return and establishment of the New Heavens and New Earth. www.reformedreader.org/mchart.htm

having become convinced that the preponderance of Scriptural evidence teaches that Christ chose me before I chose Him. Rest assured, my transition was neither sudden nor flippant. I actually fought the shift for years because of Calvinism's support of infant sprinkling. I figured if Calvinists could not accurately determine the meaning of a simple a word like "baptism"[4] then how could one trust their perspective on ideas as complicated as predestination and free-will? Nevertheless, an error in one element of a theological system does not necessarily falsify the entire theology. Just to be clear, readers should understand that my support of Calvinism does not extend to include Reformed[5] or Presbyterian theology *in toto*. It simply centres on the doctrines of Grace as defined by The Calvinist Tulip, Total Depravity, Unconditional Election, Limited Atonement, Irresistible Grace, and Perseverance of the Saints.[6] So to prevent tarnishing Reformed theology with an anti-land view, I will use the term "replacement theology" to designate the view that rejects the continued validity of the Jews' right to the land that was promised to Abraham (Gen 12, 15).

Before delving into the controversy concerning Israel's right to the Promised Land, a word of caution should be heard. I think it

---

[4] The religious movement known as Presbyterianism, which traces its heritage to Calvin, expresses baptism by sprinkling. In contrast, Greek Orthodox Christians understand the meaning of baptism as demonstrated by their immersing their infants in the waters of baptism.

[5] Reformed theologians are also known as covenant theologians.

[6] I am pleased to learn that premillennial views of eschatology, while not common, are concordant with Covenantal views. Barry E. Horner, *Future Israel: Why Christian Anti-Judaism Must Be Challenged*, ed. E. Ray Clendenen, Nac Studies in Bible & Theology, vol. 3 (Nashville: B&H Academic, 2007), 88. See also Willem A. VanGemeren, 'Israel as the Hermeneutical Crux in the Interpretation of Prophecy (Ii),' in *Westminster Theological Journal* 46, no. 2 (1984), 254-5 who states that Calvin did not have a clear theology on Israel's place in eschatology and observes that some Reformed theologians in the 17th century looked for Israel's restoration to the land (p. 257).

is essential that readers recognise that the debate over Israel's right to the land is essentially a hermeneutical conflict.[7] In other words, advocates on both sides of the debate, though sharing similar views of Scripture, disagree with how that Scripture should be interpreted. On one side, replacement theologians adopt a typological reading of Scripture and therefore tend to read Old Testament eschatological prophecies concerning Israel as ultimately being fulfilled in and through the Church. The people of God in the Old Testament are called Israel, but in the New Testament they are called the Church. On the other, non-replacement theologians take a more direct reading of Scripture and therefore tend to keep Israel and the Church as separate covenantal entities. The upshot of this is the importance in recognising that one's hermeneutical preference will significantly determine whether one adopts a replacementist or non-replacementist view of Israel. Acknowledgement of interpretation's role does not mean the answer is pre-determined. It just means that there are differences between the two positions that are so foundational to one's understanding of Scripture that to change positions requires one to reorient fundamentally his/her approach to Scripture. It also means that the answers are not as clear or obvious as dogmatists on both sides of the controversy would like us to believe because our preferred hermeneutical model biases our perception of the scriptural data. It is similar to two people, one wearing red glasses and the other blue, each trying to convince the other that the flower before them is red or blue respectively. As heated as our opinion regarding Israel's right to the land may become, we must remember that this is a fight between fellow Christians. I do not believe that one's salvation is determined by one's convictions in this area. In other words, Christians can (and do) disagree over the status of Israel's right to the land without losing their status as faithful followers of Christ.

---

[7] Norman L. Geisler, *Church, Last Things*, 4 vols. Systematic Theology, vol. 4 (Minneapolis, MN: Bethany House, 2005), 413-458. Geisler provides an excellent introduction to the issue.

As noted above, Replacement theologians argue that the Old Testament promises to Israel are transferred to the church. All Old Testament prophecies regarding Israel's right to the land, and other elements of her national life, should be interpreted in figurative or typological terms awaiting their fulfilment in the New Covenant. Replacement theologians contend that the predictions concerning Israel were ultimately fulfilled in the person of Christ. Christ, in effect, became Israel and since the Church is the body of Christ, the Church is the new Israel. So when replacement theologians read Genesis 12:1-3 and 15:13-21 they believe those promises were universalised into the Church. They base their understanding on three inter-related points.[8]

First, they contend that the Church has replaced Israel because her disobedience voided the old covenant requiring God to make a new one (Jer 31:31-2). Any chance Israel had to restore her position in the old covenant and retain its promise of land was demolished when she rejected her Messiah (Mt 21:37-45; Mk 12:1-12; Lk 20:9-19).[9]   In fact, some replacement theologians contend Paul actually acknowledges that God has rejected Israel for all eternity (1 Thess 2:14-16).[10] Second, Israel's special status before God is no longer in effect because Christ eliminated ethnic distinctions in the New Covenant. They cite Paul, who said that in

---

[8] I am relying heavily on the paper presented by Robert L. Reymond, 'Who Are the Real Heirs to the Land Promises of Holy Scripture?' in *Advancing Reformation Truth and Spirituality (ARTS)* (Fort Lauderdale, FL: Coral Ridge Presbyterian Church, 2006). Although written from an Adventist position, see also Hans K. LaRondelle, *The Israel of God in Prophecy: Principles of Prophetic Interpretation*, Andrews University Monographs, Studies in Religion, vol. XIII (Berrien Springs, MI: Andrews University Press, 1983).

[9] In the parable, the landowner represents God, the vineyard, Israel (Isa 5:7), and the farmers, the leaders. Reymond claims that the language in Mt. 21:37 and Mk 12:6 suggests that God was giving Israel one final chance to obey His commands.

[10] Reymond, 9. See also Horner, 37-38 who finds this interpretation in *The Seed of Abraham* (c. 1950) by A. Pieters.

Christ there is neither Jew nor Greek (Gal 3:28), circumcision or uncircumcision (Gal 6:15). Gentiles are no longer to be excluded from the Commonwealth of Israel (Eph 2:12). God, they claim, is no longer interested in your heritage; He is only concerned with your relationship to His son, Jesus Christ. Furthermore, replacement theologians maintain that continued emphasis on ethnic distinctions between Jew and Gentile undermines our unity created in Christ. For additional support, they point out that the New Testament writers identify the Church as the new Israel by their re-appropriating Old Testament terminology for the Church as Peter did in 1 Peter 2:9.[11] The logic is flawless. If Israel no longer retains its identity as the people of God then, in like manner, she forfeits any right to land.

Finally, replacement theologians ask if the issue of Israel's right to the land was so important, why were the Apostles so silent on the subject? Why does the New Testament only speak of land in a global and not localised manner as would be expected if Israel had a continued right to the land? In Romans 4:13, Paul converts the promise of Abraham's right to Canaan to his inheritance of the whole world.[12] Replacement theologians conclude that since Old Testament Israel becomes the Church in the New, notions of Israel's right to the land become irrelevant. For how can a nation that has been absorbed, or perhaps universalised, into the Church have the right to a particular plot of land when the Church will inherit the entire world?[13]

---

[11] Isa 61:6; Ex 19:6. See also the parallel between Isa 65:17 and 2 Pet 3:12-13 New Heavens and Earth.

[12] LaRondelle, 141.

[13] To make the matter more complicated Moshe Weinfield, *The Promise of the Land: The Inheritance of the Land of Canaan by the Israelites*, The Taubman Lectures in Jewish Studies (Berkeley: University of California Press, 1993), 214-215 finds Josephus and Philo transferring the idea of Israel's right to Palestine to Israel's right to the whole world (Ant 1:282: 4:114-116; Book of Jubilees 32:18-19).

EVALUATION

At first glance, the replacement argument is quite compelling. Replacement theologians are correct to believe that Israel is under judgment and that Gentiles are saved through the work of Jesus Christ. Additionally, Christ is the centre of the New Testament and the fulfilment of Old Testament prophecy (Lk 18:31ff; 24:27; Jn 1:45; Acts 3:18). Despite these commendable positions, replacement theology suffers from problems that fall into two broad categories.

The first category centres on the overall approach taken by the replacement theologians. Academics are frequently accused of turning simple ideas into complicated ones. While undeniable, it is also true that academics love theories that explain everything in a simple way.[14] What could be simpler than replacement theology's view that says all eschatological prophecies pertaining to Israel in the Old Testament actually apply to the Church? I am not arguing that simplicity makes replacement theology wrong. Rather, I am suggesting that it is rare for a simple theory to account for all of the biblical data. It is analogous to a police detective who is more concerned with wrapping up a case rather than making sure that his theory of the crime accounts for all the available evidence while discounting alternative theories. In other words, good theology must consider alternative theories of the evidence as well as carefully consider the possibility that it may have ignored the significance of some data simply because it did not fit the established theory.[15] Proper theological method must avoid tunnel

---

[14] Gardener speaks of how the coherence of a theory (or its beauty) can convince people to adopt it, Howard Gardner, *Changing Minds: The Art and Science of Changing Our Own and Other People's Minds* (Cambridge, MA: Harvard Business School Publications, 2006). See also Thomas Kuhn, *The Structure of Scientific Revolutions*, Third ed. (Chicago, IL: University of Chicago Press, 1996), and Horner, 292.

[15] Cf. Paul Feyerabend, *Against Method*, Revised ed. (New York: Verso, 1988).

vision. We do not need to have exhaustive knowledge; I doubt we will ever have enough information to come to a definitive conclusion (at least on this side of eternity). But we can strive for and obtain knowledge of sufficient weight and value to arrive at a responsible conclusion based upon the preponderance of all the evidence.

The other global difficulty with replacement theology lies in its rejection of direct (commonly referred to as literal) fulfilment of Old Testament prophecies related to Israel. I have already noted how replacement theologians interpret many Old Testament prophecies as typological. The problem with this perspective is that it raises questions about what the original audience understood when those prophecies took place. Consider the Abrahamic covenant (Gen 12:1-3 and 15:13-21). God promised Abraham that he would: receive an heir, obtain a reputation, be a blessing, and receive land. All Christians agree that the first three promises were literally fulfilled. Jesus was a Jew, a physical descendent of Abraham (Mt. 1:1). Jesus would be a blessing to many nations, and Jesus would give Abraham a great reputation because Abraham became known as the father of the faith (Rom 4:16). But why do the replacement theologians deny that the Jews would receive the land of Canaan? Is it not possible that Jesus could be a Davidic King over the physical land of Israel, while simultaneously ruling the nations with a rod of iron as prophesied in Psalm 2? Furthermore, do we really think that David (2 Sam 7), and Micah (Micah 4:1-5:2) and other prophets conceived a future Davidic kingdom in only a spiritualised or globalised sense? In other words, did they really believe that God's promise to give Abraham's physical descendants particular land boundaries was an optional promise?[16]

---

[16] For a defence of a literal fulfilment of the land promise to Israel see Walter C. Kaiser, Jr., "The Promised Land: A Biblical-Historical View," *Bibliotheca Sacra* 138, no. 552 (1981), Jeffrey L. Townsend, "Fulfillment of the Land of Promise in the Old Testament," *Bibliotheca*

With that question in mind let us turn to the second category of problems for replacement theologians, namely the inadequacies of their three arguments. They assert that Jeremiah 31:31-2 states that the Old Covenant containing Israel's right to the land has ended. The problem with this interpretation is that Jeremiah was proclaiming the demise of the Mosaic covenant[17] not the Abrahamic covenant, which contained God's promise of Land. Observe that in 31:35-7, God declares that His promise to Israel will end when the sun and stars stop shining, in other words, never. Lest one think that Israel will be a landless nation, Jeremiah 31:38 says that God will restore Jerusalem and that it will be established as His holy city, which will be immune from conquest. 1 Thessalonians 2:14-16 does not help the replacement theologians either. As the context shows, Paul is not condemning Jews in general but only those Jews who are actively opposing the Gospel of Christ.[18] To suggest that Paul was condemning Jews comprehensively flies not only in the face of the 1 Thessalonian testimony, but also that of Acts 17:2-5, which explicitly tells us that some Thessalonian Jews accepted Christ.

In their second argument, replacement theologians claim that ethnic identity carries no standing in the New Covenant (Gal 3:28; Eph 2:11-22). Thus if national Israel no longer bears any theological significance than it can no longer have any claim to a geographical heritage. The problem with this interpretation lies in its misunderstanding the force of the Apostle's testimony. Jews in the first century believed Gentiles had to become Jews (i.e.

Sacra 142, no. 568 (1985), 324-329. Both also discuss problems and possible solutions with the precise boundaries of the promise.

[17] LaRondelle, 143. Even LaRondelle recognises that it was the Mosaic covenant being superseded.

[18] Abraham J. Malherbe, *The Letters to the Thessalonians: A New Translation with Introduction and Commentary*, ed. William Foxwell Albright and David Noel Freedman, The Anchor Bible, vol. 32B (New York: Doubleday, 2000), 174-9. Malherbe also states that Paul was involved in an intra-Jewish polemic.

children of Abraham) in order to gain salvation. To be saved required one to become ethnically Jewish, with all the requirements of circumcision and Mosaic Law keeping entailed in that notion. The problem, as already mentioned, was that by the New Testament period Israel had made salvation (righteousness before God) a combination of ethnicity and obedience to the Law. That is why the New Testament records Christ telling Jews that their lineage to Abraham is not as significant as they think it is. Christ asserts that God could cause stones to be the children of Abraham (Mt 3:9 and parallels). God intended Israel to be the vehicle of salvation, not the destination of salvation. Consider how Christ told the Samaritan woman, "salvation is of the Jews" (Jn 4:22) and how He described the future state of glory in terms of the patriarchs and the Kingdom of Heaven (Mt 8:11). The New Testament separates salvation from race and the Law of Moses. But because the notion of race and law was so tied together with salvation and God's blessing, New Testament writers go to great lengths to show that Gentiles and Jews constitute the People of God (apart from the Law) when they follow Christ. Christ is the barrier breaker. In Christ, we are a chosen people, a holy nation.[19] That is why it says the Gentiles have been adopted, that we have become children of Abraham by faith, not genetics or obedience to the law. Paul declares that Abraham is the father of all who believe (Rom 4:11-12). Galatians 3:29 says that all who belong to Christ are the seed of Abraham. Abraham could rejoice when he saw Christ (John 8:56) because he knew that Christ would be the means through whom all promises to him (described in Genesis 12 and 15) would be fulfilled. Certainly, the Gentiles had to repent of their immoral behaviour. They needed to love the true God with all their hearts and their neighbours as themselves. But they did not have to become circumcised and adopt Jewish customs. The

---

[19] While appreciating Horner's argument that 1 Peter was written primarily to benefit Christian Jews, I contend that 1 Peter was written to converted Gentiles also in order to emphasise the unity and equality of Jews and Gentiles in Christ, Horner, 285-290.

Apostles had to correct their compatriots that their Abrahamic lineage and obedience to the Law of Moses did not grant them an automatic pass to salvation nor did Gentiles have to become Jews (through circumcision) in order to become children of Abraham.

First century Jews were wrong in this view for two reasons. First, faith, not works, justified one before God (Gen 15:6, Hab 2:4). The Old Testament did not require Gentiles to become Jews by adopting the laws of Moses as demonstrated by the conversion of Naaman, the Syrian general (2 Kgs 5:1-14), and Nineveh, during Jonah's revival. Gentiles only had to forsake idolatry and the immorality that accompanied it and worship the true God of Israel. God's purpose for Israel was that she would be a light to the Gentiles (Isa 42:6f). Remember, many of the laws of Moses could only be fulfilled if one lived in the land of Palestine. If you lived elsewhere then there was no way to obey them. Those laws were in a sense geographically and I would argue even temporally limited in their scope.[20] Once we understand what the Apostles had to confront, we can immediately recognise how many of the passages that appear to downplay the Law and Jewish cultural practices were simply the Apostles' attempt to clarify that faith, not genetics or behaviour, was the proper basis for salvation.[21]

Nevertheless, while ethnicity has no value in salvation, it is not irrelevant. Just as gender distinctions remain important after Christ[22], so also ethnicity remains important. For although Gentiles are adopted as children of Abraham, the New Testament still speaks of Jews as ethnically identifiable as demonstrated by the circumcision of Timothy (Acts 16:3) and Paul's Nazirite vow (Acts 18:18). Even the compromise at the Jerusalem Council (Acts

---

[20] I remember reading this point in an article in the Westminster Theological Journal but regret not being able to find it.

[21] For detailed reviews of relative passages consult Arnold G. Fruchtenbaum, *Israelology: The Missing Link in Systematic Theology* (Tustin, CA: Ariel Ministries, 1994, 2001).

[22] Horner, 242.

15) reaffirmed ethnic distinctions as it provided a way for Jewish and Gentile believers to maintain positive relations through cultural sensitivity. Put another way, I as an American, share a faith in Christ with believers in England. But there are cultural elements to being British that I just do not share, such as eating black pudding. In Christ, this distinction in cultural dietary tradition is irrelevant. But I would think that to be British, one's attitude toward black pudding would be strikingly different than that held by most Americans. So it is with Jewish/Gentile believers. Paul had to demonstrate that the Law of Moses did not save anyone, Jew or otherwise. But just as culture is not important for salvation nor is it something that necessarily must be condemned. Thus in Christ, Jews and Gentiles are one. But that oneness does not negate God's promise to the physical descendants of Abraham. Jews still had a role in eschatology.

To support this consider the following. First, note Christ's response to the disciples' question recorded in Acts 1:6. The setting is just prior to Christ's ascension into heaven. The disciples finally accept that Christ had come from the dead and were wondering whether Christ would now establish the Davidic Kingdom. Christ responds "It is not for you to know times or seasons that the Father has fixed by his own authority" (Acts 1:7). The question is, "Why didn't Christ rebuke the disciples and tell them that the promise of a Jewish kingdom has been voided?" I contend that Christ's failure to take up this opportunity to correct His disciples stemmed from His desire to fulfil His promise that they would sit on the thrones of Israel (Mt 19:28). In other words, the establishment of the kingdom was still to come, otherwise there would be no Israel for the disciples to rule. Those who assert that Christ's comments were metaphorically referring to the Church are guilty of special pleading. For one would have to wonder what words Jesus would have had to use to make the point clearer, namely that the state of Israel would exist one day.

Of course, one would be remiss to neglect Paul's conversation in Romans 9 to 11, which detail Israel's failure to follow Christ.

Nevertheless, Paul says God hasn't rejected his people. From the replacement perspective, it begs the question, "How can God even consider rejecting or not rejecting his people if they can no longer be identified after Christ's death and resurrection?" The problem for replacement theologians is that Paul's comments assume physical descendants of Abraham can be identified, and that they matter to God in a way that ordinary Gentiles do not.[23]

It seems to me this notion of becoming part of the people of God is what God had in mind by offering salvation to the Gentiles. The Gentiles are being blessed with fellowship with God through the Holy Spirit to make the Jews jealous by making them recall their own special relationship with God. The distinction is that I as a Gentile am grafted in to the tree of Israel by faith. What this means is that I have the opportunity to share in God's blessings and fellowship. But this doesn't mean I have the right to the land of Israel. God clearly gives certain ethnic groups their own land. Note Paul's comment in Acts 17:26. When speaking before the philosophers at the Areopagus, Paul says (and I paraphrase), that God made from one person all the nations of the earth and has determined the boundaries of their habitation. Now you could argue that Paul is just arguing from concession. But I think Paul could have proffered this notion because he knew that God would ultimately fulfil the promise of the land to Israel as God promised.

We must ultimately remember a few things:

1. God owns the land. Lev. 25:23: "The land shall not be sold in perpetuity; for the land is mine; for you are strangers and sojourners with me."

2. The land is special to God and Israel's right to it is not linked merely to her obedience to the biblical commandments. The Torah understands the Israelite victory as succeeding in part because the land itself was so holy that it vomited out the inhabitants who

---

[23] Ibid., 292ff.

defiled it by their abominable practices (Lev 18:28; Deut 9:4–5; Zech 2:14; Psa 78:54).

3. God's promise of Israel's right to the land cannot be broken. Even their failure to obey His commands will not negate the promise (Deut 9:24–29). In every prophetic message the prophecy of judgment and doom is tempered by the prophecy of consolation and restoration. Like the dry bones in Ezekiel's vision (Ezek 37:1–14), the old community of Israel will be restored, and from it the future generations will grow and flourish. The land will be cleansed of its pollution and sin and will welcome home its scattered people and become repopulated. Isaiah announces a second exodus through the wilderness to the Promised Land. God, who had "exiled" Himself along with his people, returns to dwell in Jerusalem (Is 52:8), the centre of the earth. The primary emphasis turned to the restoration of the temple and its cult and the rebuilding of the city of Jerusalem.[24]

4. The destruction of Jerusalem in A.D. 70 was God's punishment for Israel's rejection of her messiah. It was a way for God to show Israel that she needed to rethink her understanding of salvation and her relationship to God. That is why Paul continues to say that the Holy Spirit was a down payment of the promise of eternal life (Eph 1:14). The Holy Spirit showed God's relationship with the Gentiles and thus His blessing upon non-Jews. The Spirit's presence, prophesied by Joel 2:28-32 was to encourage jealousy among the Jews and goad them to repent and return to God (Rom 9-11).

What should be said about replacement theology's third point regarding the relative silence about Israel's continued right to the

---

[24] For details, see the article "Temple, Jewish" in Stanley E. Porter and Craig A. Evans, *Dictionary of New Testament Background: A Compendium of Contemporary Biblical Scholarship*, electronic ed. (Downers Grove, IL: InterVarsity Press, 2000).

land? Arguments from silence are fraught with difficulties. Although Acts 1:6-7 demonstrate that the New Testament was not silent about Israel's right to the land, I do agree that the subject was not a central one for the New Testament. Nevertheless, the relative silence of the New Testament regarding the land lacks argumentative force. Perhaps the easiest answer is that the Apostles had to be discreet about Israel's right to the land out of concern for how Rome would interpret such a message.[25] Boldly proclaiming Israel's right to the land could have easily resulted in a military reaction along the lines of Hadrian's quelling of the Bar-Kokhba Revolt.[26] More importantly, we must state that the New Testament does not deny Israel's right to the land. There is nothing in the New Testament which tells us that God's promise to Abraham is no longer valid (Gen 15:18). To the Apostles there was no need to belabour the issue because they knew God would keep His promise to Abraham. As a Calvinist who emphasises God's decrees, I can think of no surer argument than that.

Excursus: The Debate over Genesis 15:18
This passage reads, 'On that day the LORD made a covenant with Abram, saying, "To your offspring I give this land, from the river of Egypt to the great river, the river Euphrates..."' What is noteworthy is the section uses the identical Hebrew word translated as "descendant" (15:13,18) in a way that clearly emphasises the genetic aspect of the meaning of descendant. In other words, God promised the land to Abraham's physical descendants, not his spiritual ones. To further emphasise the ethnic particularity of the promise, note how God distinguished

---

[25] Paul ignored the restoration of the Israelite kingdom not because it was irrelevant but because its introduction had to wait for the Lord's return. Contra Weinfield, 178-179.
[26] Werner Eck, 'Hadrian's Hard-Won Victory: Romans Suffer Severe Losses in Jewish War,' in *Biblical Archeology Review* (September-October 2007), 44.

Abraham's descendants from the Egyptians. God did not give Israel the right to have the land of Egypt because God gave the Nile region to the Egyptians. By limiting Israel's right to certain land, God's promise of Canaan to Israel is further clarified.

Replacement theologians employ two arguments to dilute the notion of Israel's right to the land. First, they assert Hebrews 11:9f says that the territory Abraham was really seeking for was a spiritual one. Reformed theologian Robert Reymond puts the matter this way:

> ... the author of Hebrews stated that the administration of redemption under the old covenant was "but a shadow of the good things to come" (Heb 10:1), so also he taught that Abraham knew that God's land promises in their fulfillment entailed something far more glorious, namely, a better and heavenly homeland whose designer and builder is God, than the land of Palestine per se that served only as the type of their fulfillment:

Reymond then quotes Hebrews 11:8-16 and continues, saying:

> Quite plainly, Abraham understood that the land promised to him actually had both its origin and its antitypical fulfillment in the heavenly, eternal reality that lay still in the future. Possession of a particular tract of land in ancient times might have significance from a number of perspectives with respect to God's redemptive working in the world, but clearly the land promise under the Abrahamic covenant served simply as a type anticipating the future reality of the coming of the messianic kingdom with the Messiah himself assuming the throne of David in heaven[27] and ruling the universe after his

---

[27] Because any throne he, as the messianic Son of David (Matt 9:27; 20:30-31; 21:9; 22:41-46; Luke 1:31-33), were to sit upon would be "the throne of David," Jesus Christ's present session at the right hand of God

> *resurrection/ascension and reigning until all his enemies have been put under his feet.[28]*

Reymond's point is obvious. Abraham's ultimate goal was the attainment of a spiritual land. We must ask, however, "Did Abraham really have *only* a spiritual view of land in mind?" I think not.[29] The land in Abraham's eyes would have been worthless if God was not with him. The city was where God would be. Abraham's goal was to be in fellowship with God. But to suggest that the land was irrelevant or was universalised to the entire world, misses the point. A city cannot exist without land. Abraham received the promise of an heir, but he did not see the fulfilment of God's promise of land. Thus he had to look forward to the day when that would occur. It is interesting to note the New Jerusalem will be coming down from heaven (Rev 21:10). Being a city, it is the place of God's indwelling accompaniment with his people. But it is not a New Hong Kong. It is a New Jerusalem, the city where God would put his name (1 Kgs 11:36), and therefore the city ties together the theme of land and fellowship with God together.[30]

Replacement theologians also support their interpretation that the land promise to Abraham was universalised to encompass the

---

has invested the throne of God in heaven with a messianic character, that is to say, God's throne is "the throne of David." And *this* Davidic throne is the throne of the only "Jerusalem" that matters today, namely, "the Jerusalem above," the glorified church of Jesus Christ (see Gal 4:26; Heb 12:22; Rev 21:9-26).

[28] 'Who Are the Real Heirs to the Land Promises of Holy Scripture?' Robert L. Reymond. An Address Delivered to "Advancing Reformation Truth and Spirituality" (ARTS), 6 on April 21, 2006. DeVos Chapel, Coral Ridge Presbyterian Church. Fort Lauderdale, Florida.

[29] Carson calls interpretations which rely on a mistaken either/or polarity a "false disjunctive" D.A. Carson, *Exegetical Fallacies* (Grand Rapids, Michigan: Baker Book House, 1984), 94-97.

[30] Horner, 250. He cites various authors noting that heavenly in Hebrews does not mean extra-terrestrial but unpolluted because God is there.

entire world by appealing to Romans 4:13. It reads, "For the promise to Abraham and his offspring that he would be heir of the world did not come through the law but through the righteousness of faith." Our understanding of "world" lies at the heart of the interpretive dispute. Reymond interprets it to mean the planet earth. While that is certainly a possibility, the lexicography and context make it unlikely. The Greek word translated 'world' (*kosmos*) occurs 9 times in Romans (Rom 1:8, 20; 3:6, 19; 4:13; 5:12,13; 11:12, 15). Only 1:20 definitely refers to the physical planet. All the remaining occurrences of *kosmos* can be interpreted as referring to human activity and not to geography. For example, in Romans 1:8, Paul says that the faith of the Romans is proclaimed throughout the whole world. Clearly, Paul is referring to the preaching of the Gospel to people and not to physical locations. Even if one says that Paul intended *kosmos* to refer to people and places, we still must ask if one is primary. Barrett's observation that Paul is probably referring to Genesis 22:18, adds further evidence for my position.[31] Even if we concede that Paul wanted *kosmos* to refer to the planet, the verse still lacks sufficient force to overthrow the view that God promised ethnic Jews the land of Israel. Paul never denies that Israel still has a right to a particular plot of land. Paul only says that Abraham would inherit the entire world. The replacement view fails to consider that a literal bestowal of land to physical descendants of Abraham can be

---

[31] C. K. Barrett, *A Commentary on the Epistle to the Romans*, ed. Henry Chadwick, Harper's New Testament Commentaries (NY: Harper & Brothers Publishers, 1957), 94. See also James R. Edwards, *Romans*, ed. W. Ward Gasque, New International Biblical Commentary, vol. 6 (Peabody, MA: Hendrickson Publishers Inc., 1992), 122-3. See Moo for an interpretation more amenable to the replacement theology, Douglas J. Moo, *The Epistle to the Romans*, ed. Ned B. Stonehouse, F. F. Bruce, and Gordon D. Fee, The New International Commentary on the New Testament (Grand Rapids, MI: William B. Eerdmans Publishing Co., 1996), 273-4.

accomplished simultaneously with the spiritual blessings that Christ will grant to Gentiles.[32]

APPLICATION

If you agree that God has eternally promised to give Canaan to Israel, what political policies should Christians support? The question is pertinent given that the modern State of Israel is not only a secular institution but also one that has restricted Christian evangelism and denied citizenship to Messianic Jews.

First, we must clearly maintain that salvation comes only through Jesus Christ. Peter when preaching in Jerusalem said that there is no other name under heaven by which we can be saved (Acts 4:10ff). Paul in Rom 9-11 acknowledged that his fellow citizens were lost without Christ. So Jews who have not accepted Christ, though remaining in covenantal relationship with God, remain under condemnation for their refusal to accept their Messiah (Jn 3:18). God has not rejected His promise to restore them to the land once the time of the Gentiles is complete.[33] Regrettably, many Jews think that following Christ means forsaking their cultural heritage. We must affirm that Jews can retain their cultural identity. Jews must only give up those elements of Judaism that contradict the teachings of Jesus Christ. Our only desire is to reaffirm Christ's words that He, and He alone is the way to the Father (Jn 14:6). Therefore Christians must press the Israeli government to allow true religious freedom in the country.

Second, Christians can choose to support the Israeli government. However, support of the Israeli government's right to exist does not mean that Christian backing constitutes a blank cheque. Just as Christians must reject the idolatrous patriotism that

---

[32] Horner, 246.
[33] Ibid., Chapter 11.

says, 'my country right or wrong', we must similarly reject the idea that Israeli policy is always right.

Third, Pro-Israel supporters must be sensitive to those Christians who believe that God has promised Jews the land, but have moral objections to Israel's policies.[34]

Fourth, I think care must be taken to properly distinguish Christian support for Jews as an ethnic people from support for the nation of Israel as a political entity. The ideas are not necessarily coterminous. While I believe God has a plan for the modern nation of Israel, the mere fact that she exists should not blind us to the possibility that the actual workings of God's prophetic plan may take a turn that is not possible for us to foresee. Christians must never be so involved in politics that they forget that their first mission is to evangelise. As a friend put it, 'First the Gospel, then politics.'[35]

---

[34] For the record, I believe there are a number of practical reasons Christians should support Israel (despite her imperfections). It is naïve to think governments can only be supported if they are perfect. Fact: Israel offers Christians far more freedom than those had in Muslim countries. If we should condemn the excesses of Israeli nationalism, then we should condemn in even harsher terms the countries surrounding Israel that are held captive by political systems enslaved by a failed religion and political ideology. I once spoke to a Muslim imam who encouraged me to consider the importance of justice. I responded in agreement and said that I knew of Jewish organisations in Israel that fought for the rights of Palestinians. I noted my ignorance of the Arab world and asked, if he was aware of any similar Muslim organisations fighting for the rights of resident Jews in the surrounding Arab countries. He just looked at me. Acknowledging how I must have caught him off guard, I gave him my card, and asked him to send the names of the organisations when he found them. Even after several years, I never received any list. The point being, that perfection is a high standard to uphold in a fallen world. I think Christians would be better served to work for sufficient justice, a justice that "works" well enough to protect life and liberty and basic rights than to be mired in the intransigence of utopian politics.

[35] Rev. John C. Rankin of the Theological Education Institute of Hartford, Connecticut has this slogan as a title for his ministry work. www.teinetwork.com/biography.html

Finally, Christians should focus on the spiritual struggles affecting these issues. God has commanded us to pray for our leaders and for the good of mankind. In the final analysis, no matter our eschatological views, Christians should be united with a fervent expectation and call of our Lord's return. We must be cautious about our criticism of those who disagree with us. Not that we shy away from conflict within the Church. However, we must be sure that our tone is moderated and our statements endeavour to assume the best of those of which we disagree. For in the end, our goal is to represent the love of Christ to a lost world. Even so, Come Lord Jesus.

CHAPTER 5

Israel and the Purposes of God
Howard Taylor

THE UNIQUENESS OF THE PEOPLE OF ISRAEL

One very significant apologetic tool for the truth of the Bible is the history of Israel. The human subject for most of the Bible (both Old and New Testaments) is the Jewish people and their history. There is no doubt that they are unique among the nations. This does not mean the individual Jew is different from other human beings, but rather as a people their story has demonstrated God's faithfulness, as recorded and prophesied in the Bible. Thus all who trust the God of the Bible can take strength from the Jewish people and their painful yet glorious history. Their story has relevance to the whole human race and this is so even if the Jewish people themselves do not recognise it.

The following quotes illustrate the uniqueness of the Jewish people as perceived by different people in recent history:

Some people like the Jews, and some do not. But no thoughtful man can deny the fact that they are, beyond any question, the most formidable and the most remarkable race which has appeared in the world.[1] Winston Churchill

The study of the history of Europe during the past centuries teaches us one uniform lesson: That the nations which received and in any way dealt fairly and mercifully with the Jew have prospered; and that the nations that have tortured and oppressed him have written out their own curse.[2] Olive Schreiner

---

[1] *Illustrated Sunday Herald,* 8 February 1920.
[2] Olive Schreiner, South African novelist, pacifist and political activist, quoted by Chief Rabbi J. H. Hertz, *A Book of Jewish Thought* (Oxford:

By the standards of others, once they had lost their country, the Jewish people should have fallen into decay long ago. But instead, uniquely [emphasis mine]*, they continued to maintain themselves as a nation, and by doing so became in the eyes of others an uncanny and frightening people.*[3] David Vital

The Jews constitute a tiny percentage of the human race. Properly the Jew ought, hardly to be heard of; but he is heard of, has always been heard of. He is as prominent on the planet as any other people, and his commercial importance is extravagantly out of proportion to the smallness of his bulk. His contributions to the world's list of great names in literature, science, art music, finance, medicine and abstruse learning are also way out of proportion to the weakness of his numbers. He has made a marvellous fight in this world, in all the ages; and has done it with has hands tied behind him. He could be vain of himself, and be excused for it. The Egyptian, the Babylon and the Persian rose, filled the planet with sound and splendour, then faded to dream-stuff and passed away; the Greek and the Roman followed, and made a vast noise, and they are gone; other peoples have sprung up and held their torch high for a time, but it burned out, and they sit in twilight now, or have vanished. The Jew saw them all, beat them all, and is now what he always was, exhibiting no decadence, no infirmities of age, no weakening of his parts, no slowing of his energies, no dulling of his alert and aggressive mind. All things are mortal but the Jew; all other

---

Oxford University Press, 1966), 177, 180. Schreiner is best known for her novel *The Story of an African Farm*, which has been acclaimed for the manner it tackled the issues of its day, ranging from agnosticism to the treatment of women.
[3] David Vital, *The Origins of Zionism* (Oxford: Oxford University Press, 1980). David Vital is Emeritus Nahum Goldmann Professor of Diplomacy at the University of Tel Aviv.

forces pass, but he remains. What is the secret of his immortality?[4] Mark Twain

The once-Marxist Russian Nikolai Alexandrovich Berdyaev came to a similar conclusion:

I remember how the materialist interpretation of history, when I attempted in my youth to verify it by applying it to the destinies of peoples, broke down in the case of the Jews, where destiny seemed absolutely inexplicable from the materialistic standpoint... Its survival is a mysterious and wonderful phenomenon demonstrating that the life of this people is governed by a special predetermination, transcending the processes of adaptation expounded by the materialistic interpretation of history. The survival of the Jews, their resistance to destruction, their endurance under absolutely peculiar conditions and the fateful role played by them in history: all these point to the particular and mysterious foundations of their destiny.[5]

The historian Barbara Tuchman also wrote:

The history of the Jews is... intensely peculiar in the fact of having given the western world its concept of origins and monotheism, its ethical traditions, and the founder of its prevailing religion, yet suffering dispersion, statelessness and ceaseless persecution, and finally in our times nearly successful genocide, dramatically followed by fulfilment of the never-relinquished dream of return to the homeland. Viewing this strange and singular history, one cannot escape the

---

[4] From an essay entitled 'Concerning the Jews', *Harper's Magazine*, March 1898. Available online at Fordham University's *Internet History Sourcebook Project*, http://www.fordham.edu/halsall/mod/1898twain-jews.html (last accessed 16 February 2009).
[5] *The Meaning of History* (London: Geoffrey Bles, 1936), 86-87. Nikolai Berdyaev was a political philosopher who later embraced religion.

impression that it must contain some special significance for the history of mankind, that in some way, whether one believes in divine purpose or inscrutable circumstance, the Jews have been singled out to carry the tale of human fate. [6]

Three Christian Views

King Louis XIV of France asked Blaise Pascal to give him proof of the supernatural. Pascal answered, 'Why, the Jews, your Majesty, the Jews.' [7] Elsewhere Pascal writes:

It is certain that in certain parts of the world we can see a peculiar people, separated from the other peoples of the world, and this is called the Jewish people ... separated from all the other peoples of the earth, who are the most ancient of all and whose history is earlier by several centuries than the oldest histories we have. .... My encounter with this people amazes me and seems worthy of attention ... Lovingly and faithfully they hand on this book in which Moses declares that they have been ungrateful towards God throughout their lives, that he knows they will be still more so after his death, but that he calls heaven and earth to witness against them that he told them so often enough. [8]

Pascal's amazement includes the observation that the Jews

---

[6] Quoted by Sir Rabbi Jonathan Sacks in *Covenant and Conversation: Thoughts on the Weekly Parsha From the Chief Rabbi*, available from the Chief Rabbi's website, www.chiefrabbi.org/thoughts/balak5765.htm (last accessed 17 February 2009). Barbara Wertheim Tuchman was an American historian and author best known for *The Guns of August*, a history of the prelude to the First World War.
[7] This quotation is cited by Rabbi Blech, Associate Professor of the Talmud at Yeshiva University, in 'The Miracle of Jewish History', *History News Network* website (George Mason University's Center for History and News Media), in http://hnn.us/articles/38887.html (last accessed 17 February 2009).
[8] Blaise Pascal, *Pensees*, 454, 452. Version cited is *Pensees* (London: Penguin, 1966). Translated by A.J. Krailssheimer.

preserve and transmit a book that is unflattering to them. This surely merits our attention. He also states:

This people are not eminent solely by their antiquity, but are also singular by their duration, which has always continued from their origin till now. For, whereas the nations of Greece and of Italy, of Lacedaemon, of Athens and of Rome, and others who came long after, have long since perished, these ever remain, and in spite of the endeavours of many powerful kings who have a hundred times tried to destroy them, as their historians testify, and as it is easy to conjecture from the natural order of things during so long a space of years, they have nevertheless been preserved (and this preservation has been foretold); and extending from the earliest times to the latest, their history comprehends in its duration all our histories which it preceded by a long time.[9]

Karl Barth, who did not like proofs from nature for the Christian faith, said of the history of the Jews:

In fact, if the question of a proof of God is raised, one need merely point to this simple historical fact. For in the person of the Jew there stands a witness before our eyes, the witness of God's covenant with Abraham, Isaac and Jacob and in that way with us all. Even one who does not understand Holy Scripture can see this reminder. And don't you see, the remarkable theological importance, the extraordinary spiritual and sacred significance of the National Socialism (Nazism) that now lies behind us is that right from its roots it was anti-Semitic, that in this movement it was realised with a simple demonic clarity, that the enemy is the Jew. Yes, the enemy in this matter had to be a Jew. In this Jewish nation there really lives to this day the extraordinariness of the revelation of God.[10]

---

[9] Pascal, 451.
[10] Karl Barth, *Dogmatics in Outline*, 75-76.

The Anglican theologian and distinguished churchman, Alan Richardson, wrote:

> *In view of the remarkable history of the Jewish people it ought not to seem strange to us that they should have some unique destiny to fulfil in the providence of God. The history of other nations provides not even a single remote parallel to the phenomenon of Jewish existence down the ages and to this day. What other nation of antiquity has preserved its identity and character as the Jews have done, though exiled from their homeland and dispersed throughout the world? Throughout centuries of persecution the Jewish race has survived the catastrophes which have so often destroyed the national identity of other peoples. Religious or secularised a Jew remains a Jew - a voluntary or involuntary witness to the truth that is symbolised in the story of God's Covenant with Abraham. This striking fact of the persistence of the Jewish race has long been recognised as important evidence of the truth of the Biblical interpretation of history* [11]

PEOPLE AND LAND

Redemption is primarily for people but also it is for the natural world. Genesis 1 is the account of how God created people and nature. Genesis 3 is about how humans sinned and brought decay to all of nature. Therefore land is not just a temporary sign (like the Temple sacrifices), rather it is part of the content of redemption.

To represent all people, God needed a Chosen People, and to represent all lands He needed a Promised Land. The relation of the Jewish people with the land which God entrusted to them

---

11 *Christian Apologetics* (London: SCM), 1947). This is an excerpt from a larger passage found in pages 141-143.

represents in 'peculiar intensity'[12] all of us and the lands which are entrusted to us.

Over and over again the Old Testament Prophets tell us that the history of the Jews will be unlike the history of any other people, and how towards the end of time, after great suffering, the Jews will return to the Promised Land where they will become the centre of hostility. This hostility will affect the whole world. Eventually God will reconcile them to their Messiah, cleanse them from their sin, judge the nations who have hated them, and make them a blessing to all peoples (for example, Isa 43, 49, Jer 30-33, Ezek 36-39, Zech 12, 13). We shall see that the New Testament confirms this Old Testament promise. Events this century seem to be fulfilling these prophecies.

There are often arguments about whether or not such verses refer to the return from Babylonian exile or even the initial entry into Canaan. To be convinced let us consider the principles that Moses gives Israel even before they enter the Promised Land for the first time.

(a) God's judgement against Israel's sin means that her people will be scattered from the land.

And the Lord will scatter you among all peoples, from one end of the earth to the other, and there you shall serve other gods of wood and stone, which neither you nor your fathers have known. And among these nations you shall find no respite, and there shall be no resting place for the sole of your foot, but the Lord will give you there a trembling heart and failing eyes and a languishing soul Your life shall hang in doubt before you. Night and day you shall be in dread and have no assurance of your life. In the morning you shall say, 'If only it were evening!' and at evening you shall say, 'If only

---

[12] Professor T. F. Torrance's often used phrase to describe the Jewish people.

it were morning!' because of the dread that your heart shall feel, and the sights that your eyes shall see. (Deut 28:64-67)

Anyone who knows anything about Jewish history - especially during the last 1000 years - will recognise these words as striking indeed. They were spoken by Moses 3,300 years ago and have been remarkably fulfilled throughout Jewish history until this present day. Even liberal Bible scholars, who deny that Moses himself spoke these words, recognise that they are at least 2,500 years old.

(b) God's forgiveness to Israel will mean that God will restore its people to the land.

Then the Lord your God will restore your fortunes and have compassion on you, and he will gather you again from all the peoples where the Lord your God has scattered you. If your outcasts are in the uttermost parts of heaven, from there the Lord your God will gather you, and from there he will take you. And the Lord your God will bring you into the land that your fathers possessed, that you may possess it. And he will make you more prosperous and numerous than your fathers. (Deut 30:3-5)

These are the principles laid down in the book of the Law and therefore do not refer only to this or that event in the history of Israel. They describe God's dealing with Israel *in all its history.* They are expounded and applied over and over again in the Hebrew Prophets (Isaiah, Jeremiah, Ezekiel, Hosea, Zechariah). Indeed they are a major theme of most of the Prophets.

Although Israel's return to the land is usually linked to their return to the Lord it must not be interpreted to mean that God's purposes are conditional on good behaviour. (If they were there would be no hope for any part of the world or for any of us personally - it is by grace we are saved.) Jeremiah 31 is one of those many marvellous passages that speak of Israel's restoration and then towards the end of the chapter we read these words:

Thus says the Lord: "If the heavens above can be measured, and the foundations of the earth below can be explored, then I will cast off all the offspring of Israel for all that they have done, declares the Lord." (verse 37)

It is true, as we have seen, that the full blessings of the covenant were dependent upon Israel's behaviour. But the fulfilment of His purposes through them and their land is not dependent upon them at all. These purposes extend to the end of time and belong to God's sovereign purposes that cannot be thwarted by man's folly (Rom 3:3-4)

But now to a very important question: does the New Testament have anything to say about the principles of scattering and re-gathering which Moses spoke of, or do these principles apply only to Old Testament times? In Luke 21:20-24 we read:

But when you see Jerusalem surrounded by armies, then know that its desolation has come near. Then let those who are in Judea flee to the mountains, and let those who are inside the city depart... for these are days of vengeance, to fulfill all that is written... *They will fall by the edge of the sword and be led captive among all nations, and Jerusalem will be trampled underfoot by the Gentiles,* until the times of the Gentiles are fulfilled. (emphasis mine)

This passage tells us that the *coming* scattering of Israel is the true fulfilment of the Old Testament prophecies. We therefore conclude these Old Testament prophecies cannot have referred only to the Babylonian exile hundreds of years before Christ! Thus, the Old Testament prophecies about the restoration after exile must also refer to events after Christ as well as events before His time on earth. This is confirmed by the last words in the above quote which show us that the coming Jewish exile from Jerusalem *is not forever.*

There is also another very interesting word from our Lord found in Matthew 24:34-35:

> *Truly, I say to you, this generation will not pass away until all these things take place. Heaven and earth will pass away, but my words will not pass away.*

What does "generation" mean in this passage? To answer this let us consider which Old Testament passage this seems to be based on. We have already referred to part of it above. Jeremiah 31 is one of the many great passages speaking of the restoration of Israel to its land in the last days. In verse 36-37 the Lord says:

> *"If this fixed order* (the rational principles of nature which make science possible) *departs from before me," declares the Lord, "then shall the <u>offspring</u> of Israel cease from being a nation before me forever." Thus says the Lord: "If the heavens above can be measured, and the foundations of the earth below can be explored, then I will cast off all the <u>offspring</u> of Israel for all that they have done, declares the Lord."*

The Greek version of the Old Testament is called the Septuagint, and it was widely used by the Jews at the time of Jesus. The Septuagint word for offspring, or "descendants", in Jeremiah 31 is the very same word that Jesus uses in Matthew 24, and which, in our New Testaments is translated "generation" from the Greek. In the Greek it is the word "genea" and literally means "family", "race" or "generation". It seems to me that Jesus is doing what He does over and over again in His teaching, namely, quoting or paraphrasing the Old Testament Scriptures. In this particular case, in saying, 'this generation will not pass away', He is confirming the promise given through Jeremiah, that in spite of all the Jews have done wrong, God will preserve them to the end of the world. Jeremiah makes this prophecy in the context of God's pledge to bring the Jews back to the Promised Land near the end of the age and Jesus sets His seal on it.

OBJECTIONS TO THE SIGNIFICANCE OF ISRAEL IN GOD'S PURPOSES

There are political as well as theological objections to the continuing significance of Israel. In this writer's view they are the overwhelming reason why the unique significance of Israel is overlooked these days. They can be summarised as follows.

Political Objections

If one sincerely believes that, in 1947-48 the Jews turned up from Europe and, with overwhelming odds, expelled much of the long standing local population and then expanded this conquest in 1967, it will be very difficult to believe that the hand of God was in such clearly unjust events.

Further if one sincerely believes that, if only Israel would withdraw to the pre-1967 boundaries, the huge Islamic world would give up its former aim of destroying Israel, then one will certainly place the blame for the continuing tragic events upon Israel. If, however, one believes an Israeli withdrawal would greatly increase its vulnerability to suicide bombs and invading armies, then one will understand why a withdrawal at this moment in time would be near suicidal. (The country would be a mere nine miles wide at its middle-populated area). If one believes that over half the Israeli population were from the Middle East and not from Europe and were fleeing Arab persecution, then one will be more sympathetic to these new immigrants. This sympathy will be strengthened if one believes the Arab nations started the 1967 war with the purpose of destroying Israel.

Theological Objections

If one believes God's relationship with his creation is purely spiritual (i.e. He does not interact with the physical space-time of this world) then one will find it difficult to believe He is active in

history so as to give the Jews a unique history among the nations –
a history which has now resulted in their re-gathering. If one does
hold this view (a form of Deism), one must still come to terms
with what is widely observed (even by the non-religious), namely
that Jewish history is remarkable in its uniqueness. If, on the other
hand, one believes God can and does act in the space-time of this
world, then they will not have a theological problem with the
uniqueness of Jewish history and perhaps its restoration to the
land.

If one believes the Old Testament is concerned with a
particular people and land and not with all the world, and that the
New Testament gives this a universal application, then one will
find it difficult to see how God could have any continuing special
purpose for Israel and its land. If, however, one believes both Old
and New Testaments hold the particular and universal together
(this is the argument of Paul in Romans 2-3 and 9-11), then one
will find it easier to see the continuing significance of land.

If one holds the view based on such texts as 1 Peter 2:9, that
the mission of ancient Israel has been *transferred* to the Church
(i.e. Replacement Theology or Supercessionism), then one will
call the Church the new Israel and one will not hold that modern
Israel has a unique significance in the purposes of God. This is
precisely the kind of conclusion that the Apostle Paul refuses to
draw at the end of Romans 2 and the beginning of Romans 3,
when discussing the relationship between the new circumcision
and the old. If on the other hand we hold that the privileges of
ancient Israel are not transferred but used merely to *describe* the
Church, then we will not have any difficulty in recognising the
continuing significance of the history of the Jewish people.

If one believes the salvation of Christ is only for the spiritual
part of human beings, then one will find it difficult to believe the
land is significant. If one believes, however, that the redemption of
Christ embraces all creation then one will be able to see that land
is significant. Since Paul (Rom 9-11) reaffirms God's ancient
covenant with Jewish Israel and that at the *heart* of this ancient

covenant is 'land', one will see why Paul does not need to refer explicitly to their restoration to the land, especially as, at that time, they were not even in exile from the land.

If one believes Christ fulfils Israel's unique destiny and that fulfilment includes in its meaning a 'putting an end to', then one will find it difficult to see the continuing relevance of Israel in the story of redemption. If, however, one believes that Christ fulfils Israel's destiny from Abraham *to the end of time,* then one will see Israel's continuing history as 'in Christ' – even if Israel itself does not recognise it.

If one believes the temple (a temporary sign of the covenant) is equivalent to the 'land', then one will believe (on the basis of the letter to the Hebrews[13]) that 'land' has lost its significance. If, however, one distinguishes between 'sign' (e.g. temple and its sacrifices) and 'content' (God, people, land) then one will see the continuing significance of land.

The Mystery of Jewish Identity

The question 'What is a Jew?' still puzzles the authorities in the State of Israel, as they agonise today over whom their 'law of return' applies. One of the points the Apostle Paul makes in Romans 9:7ff is that ethnicity – mere physical descent from the patriarchs – was never a guarantee of belonging to the people of Israel. He uses the examples of Ishmael and Esau who were not seen as part of the chosen people, even though they were descended from Abraham to whom God's call and promise were given. The Hebrew Scriptures also record numerous examples of people who were not physically descended from Jacob being counted as Israelites, for example Ruth, Uriah the Hittite, Hushai the Archite, and many others. This is still true today: Israel is one of the most racially mixed nations in the world. As the whole Bible makes clear, families include adopted children who are to be regarded of the same worth and given the same privileges as their natural children.

---

[13] For example, Hebrews 8:13.

If we cannot define a Jew in racial terms, neither can we do so by looking to religion. Many Jews today are secular. Even historically we would not be able to identify Jews just by their religious beliefs and practices. The Hebrew Scriptures are quite clear that there were many Jews who rejected and effectively rebelled against the God of their fathers.

So, although it is difficult to push Jewishness into a pigeonhole of race or religion, it cannot be denied that the Jewish identity has existed distinctively for thousands of years and continues to endure today. Jewishness is a startling fact of world history. In the letter to the believers in Rome, in which Paul discusses the history of the identity of God's people, he explains 'it does not depend on human will or effort, but on God's mercy'[14]. In other words, we cannot define Jewishness. It is something sustained by the grace of God. The extraordinary persistence of the distinct Jewish people provides the lesson that, good or bad, we live only by God's grace.

Death of Christ

Who was responsible for the death of Christ? Often, but not always, the Orthodox, the Roman Catholics and the Lutherans have described the death of Jesus as the death of a martyr.

The New Testament, while not excusing the human perpetrators of the deed, presents it, primarily, as a sacrifice of atonement, purposed by God. In his letter to the Romans, Paul struggles with the following conundrum: God elected Israel, yet they rejected the Messiah. However, God purposed that they reject the Messiah, so that the Gentile world would be forgiven through the death of Christ. In other words, they were *disobedient for our sake*[15]. Therefore what is the relationship between the Church and Jewish Israel? Paul's answer is that God's purposes for Israel still continue and the Church must behave well towards Israel or else it will be held responsible for their unbelief.

---

[14] Romans 9:16.
[15] For example, Romans 11:28.

CHAPTER 6

Jealous For Zion: Evangelicals, Zionism and the Restoration of Israel

Paul Wilkinson

And the word of the Lord of hosts came, saying, "Thus says the Lord of hosts: I am jealous for Zion with great jealousy, and I am jealous for her with great wrath. Thus says the Lord: I have returned to Zion and will dwell in the midst of Jerusalem, and Jerusalem shall be called the faithful city, and the mountain of the Lord of hosts, the holy mountain". (Zech. 8:1-3).

According to Edward Flannery, without Christian support for Zionism 'it is highly unlikely that the present State of Israel would have come into being so rapidly as it did'.[1] Lawrence Epstein concurs, suggesting that too few people appreciate 'how much Christians have contributed to the Zionist movement and to the nation of Israel'.[2] In 1985, Israel's ambassador to the United Nations, Benjamin Netanyahu, gave the following tribute at a prayer breakfast in Washington DC:

I suggest that for those who know the history of Christian involvement in Zionism, there is nothing either surprising nor new about the steadfast support given to Israel by believing Christians all over the world. For what, after all, is Zionism but the fulfilment of ancient prophecies?...There was an ancient yearning in our common tradition for the return of the Jews to the Land of Israel. And this dream, smouldering through two millennia, first burst forth in the Christian

---

[1] Edward H. Flannery, 'Christian Zionist Ethos should be Revived', *Providence Journal-Bulletin* (26 April 1996), http://nclci.org/Articles/art-flan-ethos.htm, 28 October 2008.

[2] Lawrence J. Epstein, *Zion's Call: Christian Contributions to the Origins and Development of Israel* (London: University Press of America, 1984), ix.

Zionism of the 19th Century – a movement that paralleled and reinforced modern Jewish Zionism...Thus it was the impact of Christian Zionism on Western Statesmen that helped modern Jewish Zionism achieve the rebirth of Israel.[3]

In a letter to the *Jerusalem Post* dated 26 October 1975, G. Douglas Young, founder of the Jerusalem-based Israel-American Institute of Biblical Studies (1959) and the Bridges for Peace ministry of reconciliation (1976), wrote the following:

Sir, – I have been accused of being a Zionist – a Christian Zionist – by some of my co-religionists in Israel and in the administered areas. I would like to take this means of thanking them for this compliment. In spite of being a Christian, my Jewish friends in Israel and elsewhere have labelled me a Christian Zionist and for this I want to thank them too...I feel sorry for my Christian friends, and apologise for some of them, who are silent and have not yet identified publicly with Zionism, perhaps because they do not understand it or because they fear other consequences.[4]

Though well attested and eulogised by Jewish and non-Jewish commentators alike, Christian support for the modern State of Israel continues to arouse strong, and sometimes furious, opposition from many quarters. Such hostility emanates not only from fanatics like Mahmoud Ahmadinejad, and the international community which has consistently failed to denounce his anti-Semitic tirades, but also, more disturbingly, from within the Church. A growing number of theologians, clergymen, and parachurch organisations have been outraged by the Christian Zionist claim that Israel's re-establishment on 14 May 1948 ought

---

[3] Benjamin Netanyahu, 'Christian Zionism and the Jewish Restoration', www.internationalwallofprayer.org/A-091-Christian-Zionism-and-the-Jewish-Restoration.html (28 October 2008).
[4] Quoted in Calvin B. Hanson, *A Gentile, With the Heart of a Jew* (Nyack, NY: Parson Publishing, 1979), 294-295.

to be attributed to the fulfilment of Biblical prophecy, and therefore to the hand of God. Their response has been to rally behind and promote the Palestinian/Arab agenda, by campaigning for divestment from Israel and by supporting the boycott of Israeli goods and universities.[5] There can be no doubt: 'Israel' has become a watershed issue for the Church.

In this chapter we will consider how Evangelical belief in the promised restoration of Israel prepared the ground theologically *and* politically for the establishment of the modern State of Israel. I will emphasise the role played by a number of prominent Evangelical leaders in Britain and the United States, and draw particular attention to the key motivating factor behind their Zionist endeavours: belief in the *imminent* return of the Lord Jesus Christ.

William E. Blackstone and the Balfour Declaration
Following a meeting of British Prime Minister Lloyd George's cabinet on 31 October 1917, a letter was written on their behalf by then Foreign Secretary Arthur James Balfour. Dated 2 November 1917, the letter declared the 'sympathy' of the British government with 'Jewish Zionist aspirations'. Viewing with favour 'the establishment in Palestine of a national home for the Jewish people', the British government resolved to 'use their best endeavours to facilitate the achievement of this object'. The letter was addressed to Lord Rothschild, a leader of the Jewish community in Britain, for the attention of the Zionist Federation. Despite the British government's subsequent, and well-documented, betrayal of the Jewish people, which was sealed on 17 March 1939 following the publication of its 'reprehensible'[6]

---

[5] For a comprehensive survey of the 'Christian Palestinianist' movement, see Paul Richard Wilkinson, *For Zion's Sake: Christian Zionism and the Role of John Nelson Darby* (Milton Keynes: Paternoster, 2007), 48-66.
[6] Douglas J. Culver, *Albion and Ariel: British Puritanism and the Birth of Political Zionism* (New York: Peter Lang, 1995), 24.

and 'unconscionable'[7] White Paper (which severely restricted Jewish immigration into 'Palestine'), the *Balfour Declaration* paved the way for Israel's re-establishment in 1948. However, without the official approval of U.S. President Woodrow Wilson, 'powerful forces in London'[8] which were opposed to the *Declaration* might have prevailed.

The Blackstone Memorial

On 30 June 1917, Thomas Woodrow Wilson (1856-1924), a 'son of the (Presbyterian) manse' from Staunton, Virginia, was presented with a petition which had originally been drawn up in November 1890, during a conference on 'The Past, Present and Future of Israel'. This unprecedented gathering of Christian and Jewish leaders at the First Methodist Episcopal Church in Chicago had been organised by William Eugene Blackstone (1841-1935), founder of the Hebrew Chicago Mission and a successful businessman turned lay preacher who had converted to Christ at the age of ten. What became known as the *Blackstone Memorial* was signed by over four hundred of America's most notable politicians, industrialists, newspaper editors, journalists, and religious leaders, and was presented to President Benjamin Harrison on 5 March 1891. The petition called upon the American administration to persuade its European counterparts to convene an international conference on behalf of the Jews. Such a conference, Blackstone maintained, would seek to alleviate the suffering of European Jewry, especially in the wake of the Russian pogroms, and consider what he believed to be the rightful claim of the Jewish people to 'Palestine' as 'their home, an inalienable possession from which they were expelled by force'[9] during the Roman occupation.

---

[7] Dave Hunt, *Judgment Day! Islam, Israel and the Nations*, 2nd edn (Bend, OR: The Berean Call, 2006), 94.
[8] Rufus Learsi, *The Jews in America: A History* (New York: The World Publishing Company, 1954), 257.
[9] 'Palestine for the Jews: Copy of Memorial presented to President

Although Blackstone's petition ultimately failed, it struck a chord some years later with one of America's leading Zionists, and close confidant of Woodrow Wilson, Supreme Court Justice Louis D. Brandeis (1856-1941). The *Memorial* was brought to the attention of Brandeis, and on 8 May 1916 a letter was sent on his behalf to Blackstone by New York businessman Nathan Straus. It included the following personal, and remarkable, tribute:

> *Mr Brandeis is perfectly infatuated with the work that you have done along the lines of Zionism. It would have done your heart good to have heard him assert what a valuable contribution to the cause your document is. In fact he agrees with me that* you are the Father of Zionism, *as your work antedates Herzl* (emphasis mine).

In July 1916, Blackstone was the guest of honour at a large Zionist meeting in Philadelphia, where Brandeis introduced him as 'a most important ally which Zionism has in America outside the Jewish rank'.[10]

Following a meeting in April 1917 with British Foreign Secretary Balfour, Brandeis decided that the best way to convince President Wilson of the need to support the British proposal for a Jewish homeland was to appeal to his 'biblically based Christian faith'.[11] Brandeis contacted William Blackstone and urged him to re-present his petition. The revised *Memorial* was finally presented on Blackstone's behalf to the President on 30 June 1917. Although Woodrow Wilson withheld his public endorsement of the petition on the grounds of political expediency, he nevertheless

Harrison, March 5th, 1891', in *Christian Protagonists for Jewish Restoration* (New York: Arno Press, 1977), 1-2.
[10] Quoted in Paul C. Merkley, *The Politics of Christian Zionism 1891-1948* (London: Frank Cass, 1998), 89, 61.
[11] Merkley, *The Politics of Christian Zionism*, 89.

authorised Brandeis to convey to Balfour and the British cabinet his 'entire sympathy'[12] with their proposal.

It is not without cause, then, that William Blackstone has been described as 'one of a handful of the most influential American actors in the story leading to the achievement of the state of Israel'.[13] As E. Schuyler English declared in a 1943 edition of *Our Hope* magazine, 'The best friend that the Jew has is the Christian, who knows God's Word, His love for His Chosen People, and their place in the prophetic plan.'[14] Blackstone was such a Christian. He is described in the *Encyclopaedia Judaica* as the 'most famous of the Zionist millenarians in the United States',[15] and in 1956 the Israeli government paid their own tribute by naming a forest in his honour.

Despite such acclaim Blackstone's Zionist legacy must be set in its proper context. The zeal he had for Zion stemmed from his zeal for the God of Zion, whose Son, he believed, was soon to return.

Jesus is Coming
In 1878, Blackstone published a 96 page pamphlet entitled, *Jesus is Coming*, which was later expanded, revised, and translated into over forty languages. In what became 'the most widely read premillennialist book of its time',[16] Blackstone demonstrated from the Scriptures how the physical and spiritual restoration of Israel was not only 'an incontrovertible fact' of Biblical prophecy, but also one that was 'intimately connected with our Lord's

---

[12] David Brog, *Standing with Israel: Why Christians Support the Jewish State* (Lake Mary, FL: FrontLine, 2006), 116-118.
[13] Merkley, *The Politics of Christian Zionism*, 60.
[14] Quoted in Arno C. Gaebelein, *The Conflict of the Ages*, Revised edn (Neptune, NJ: Loizeaux Brothers, 1983), xv.
[15] *Encyclopaedia Judaica* (Jerusalem: Keter Publishing House Ltd, c.1971), 16, 1154.
[16] Timothy P. Weber, *Living in the Shadow of the Second Coming: American Premillennialism, 1875-1982* (Chicago, IL: University of Chicago Press, 1987), 137.

appearing'. To detractors in the Church he made the following appeal:

> *But, perhaps, you say: 'I don't believe the Israelites are to be restored to Canaan, and Jerusalem rebuilt.' Dear reader! have you read the declarations of God's word about it? Surely nothing is more plainly stated in the Scriptures...We beg of you to read them thoroughly. Divest yourself of prejudice and preconceived notions, and let the Holy Spirit show you, from His word, the glorious future of God's chosen people, 'who are beloved' (Rom.11:28), and dear unto Him as 'the apple of His eye' (Zech.2:8).*[17]

In front of a large Zionist gathering in Los Angeles on 27 January 1918, Blackstone explained that his solidarity with the Zionist movement was based on his firm belief that 'true Zionism is founded on the plan, purpose, and fiat of the everlasting and omnipotent God, as prophetically recorded in His Holy Word, the Bible.'[18] Some years earlier he had despaired at Theodor Herzl's indifference towards 'Palestine', when Herzl was seeking to secure a viable homeland for the Jewish people. Blackstone duly sent Herzl a Bible, with all the prophecies pertaining to the Land of Israel clearly marked for his attention. By 1932, Blackstone was in no doubt: 'God's hand is in this [Zionist] movement.'

Despite his Biblical convictions and his solidarity with the Jewish people, Blackstone's focus was not on Israel, however dear to God and central to His purposes he understood that nation to be. It is precisely because his focus lay not on Zion, but on the God of Zion, that he was able to articulate a clear and appropriate *Christian* response to the question of Israel's national future, and play such a crucial role in the securing of a national home for the

---

[17] William E. Blackstone, *Jesus is Coming* (Chicago, IL: Fleming H. Revell Company, 1932), 176, 162.

[18] David A. Rausch, *Zionism within early American Fundamentalism 1878-1918* (New York: The Edwin Mellen Press, 1979), 268.

Jewish people. Blackstone's attention was firmly fixed on the Second Coming of Jesus Christ, who, he believed, would first appear to catch away His Church (1 Thess. 4:15-18), before returning, at least seven years later, to take up His earthly throne as King in Zion (cf. Psa. 2:6-7; Isa. 9:6-7; Zech. 9:9). Time was short, he believed, both for unbelievers who had thus far rejected Christ, *and* for those in the Church who had lost sight of His return. As he wrote in the opening pages of his book:

> *Reader, do you know that Jesus is coming again? He said, 'I will come again' (John 14:3) and His word endureth forever, for He is the truth...Perhaps you are not a Christian, and say – 'I don't care anything about it.' Then, dear friend, we point you to the crucified Saviour as the only hope of salvation...He is coming, and we know neither the day, nor the hour, when He may come. What if He should come now? Would you be found of Him in peace, or would you be left behind to endure the terrible things which shall come upon the world, while the church is with Christ in the air?*

In the same way that faithful Jews like Simeon and Anna had been watching and waiting immediately prior to Christ's *first* advent (Lk. 2:25-39), so in Blackstone's day 'many of the most devout and faithful of God's people...in this and foreign lands' had become 'seriously impressed with the conviction, that the coming of the Lord is near'.[19] As we shall see in due course, the man Blackstone was perhaps indebted to more than any other for his premillennial understanding of Israel's restoration and his pretribulational understanding of Christ's return, was an 'Irish clergyman'[20] by the name of John Nelson Darby.

---

[19] Blackstone, *Jesus is Coming*, 242, 11-13, 213.
[20] Francis W. Newman, *Phases of Faith* (London: Trübner & Co., 1881), 17.

The Church's Duty to Israel

During the nineteenth century a number of Evangelicals in Britain were instrumental in recovering the Church's historic, *premillennial* faith, after centuries of amillennial and postmillennial heterodoxy. The theological seed had been sown by a number of English Puritans during the seventeenth century, including Sir Henry Finch (c.1558-1625), whose book, *The Worlds Great Restauration, or The Calling of the Jewes, and with them of all the Nations and Kingdomes of the Earth, to the Faith of Christ* (1621), sent shockwaves throughout the political and ecclesiastical world because of its emphasis on Israel's *national* restoration. The seed was subsequently watered during the Evangelical Revival of the eighteenth century, when John and Charles Wesley led the way in reviving interest in Biblical prophecy, and with it, concern for the present and future prospect of the Jewish people. However, it was not until a period of unprecedented political and economic upheaval in Europe inspired premillennialist scholars such as James Bicheno, James Hatley Frere, and George Stanley Faber to turn the attention of the Church back to Biblical prophecy, that Israel's place on the theological and eschatological map came into sharper focus.[21]

On 17 November 1839, following his return from a Church of Scotland mission of inquiry to 'Palestine', the young Presbyterian minister, Robert Murray McCheyne (1813-1843), preached a sermon entitled, 'Our Duty to Israel'. Based on his key text, Rom. 1:16, McCheyne stressed how critically important it was for the Church not only to preach the Gospel 'first to the Jew', but also to experience God's compassion for His ancient covenant people. He gave the following impassioned plea to the Church, which resonated throughout much of the Evangelical world during the nineteenth century:

---

[21] See Wilkinson, *For Zion's Sake*, 135-201.

> The cloud of indignation and wrath that is even now
> gathering above the lost will break first upon the head of
> guilty, unhappy, unbelieving Israel. And have you none of the
> bowels of Christ in you, that you will not run first to them
> that are in so sad a case?...It is like God to care first for the
> Jews. It is the chief glory and joy of a soul to be like
> God...But the whole Bible shows that God has a peculiar
> affection for Israel...Strange, sovereign, most peculiar love!
> He loved them because He loved them...Now the simple
> question for each of you is, and for our beloved Church,
> Should we not share with God in His peculiar affection for
> Israel? If we are filled with the Spirit of God, should we not
> love as He loves? Should we not grave Israel upon the palms
> of our hands, and resolve that through our mercy they also
> may obtain mercy?[22]

The hub of this burgeoning, philo-Semitic, Restorationist movement was the London Society for the Promotion of Christianity amongst the Jews (LSPCJ). Founded in 1809, the London Jews Society, as it was more commonly known, drew into its fold such notable Evangelicals as William Wilberforce, Lewis Way, Alexander McCaul, Charles Simeon, Hugh McNeile, J.C. Ryle, and Alfred Edersheim. Another long-time advocate, and future president of the LSPCJ, was the eminent Christian philanthropist and seventh Earl of Shaftesbury, Anthony Ashley Cooper (1801-1885).

Conscious of His Coming
Shaftesbury was convinced that Britain had been sovereignly appointed by God to help the Jewish exiles return to their promised land. He successfully persuaded his stepfather-in-law, Lord Palmerston, to establish a British consulate in Jerusalem, and was instrumental in the establishment of the first Protestant

---

[22] Andrew A. Bonar, *Memoir and Remains of Robert Murray McCheyne* (Edinburgh: The Banner of Truth Trust, 1978), 490-493.

Bishopric in that city. The appointment of the converted Rabbi, Michael Solomon Alexander, as first Anglican Bishop of Jerusalem, owed much to Shaftesbury's influence.[23] According to an article which appeared in *The Times* newspaper in 1839, Lord Shaftesbury 'turned public attention to the claims which the Jewish people still have upon the land of Israel as their rightful inheritance'.[24] As one biographer records,

> *'Oh, pray for the peace of Jerusalem!' were the words engraven on the ring he always wore on his right hand – the words, too, that were engraven on his heart. His study of the prophetic Scriptures led him to associate the return of the Jews with the Second Advent of our Lord, and this was the hope that animated every other.*[25]

As Hodder's quote suggests, Shaftesbury's zeal for Zion cannot be understood in isolation, for it was the hope of Christ's return that motivated his Zionist endeavours. As he himself confessed towards the end of his life,

> *I think I can say that, for the last forty years, I have not lived one conscious hour that was not influenced by 'the Hope' of the Coming again of the Lord Jesus Christ.*[26]

Shaftesbury was not alone. Another respected churchman who understood the centrality to the Christian faith of Christ's return and Israel's restoration was the first Anglican Bishop of Liverpool, J.C. Ryle (1816-1900). In his sermon, 'Scattered Israel to be Gathered', Ryle declared that the denial of these two truths was 'as astonishing and incomprehensible to my own mind as the

---

[23] See Wilkinson, *For Zion's Sake*, 211-216.

[24] *The Times*, 24 January (1839), 3.

[25] Edwin Hodder, *The Life and Work of the Seventh Earl of Shaftesbury, K.G., Vol. II* (London: Cassell & Company Ltd., 1886), 477.

[26] Quoted in Maud E. Powell, *'Maranatha' (Our Lord is Coming)*, 2nd edn (London: Samuel E. Roberts, 1913), 13.

denial of the divinity of Christ.' There was, however, an order of priority for the Church, as Ryle explained:

> *The one point on which I desire to fix the eyes of my own soul, is the second personal coming of my Lord and Saviour Jesus Christ. To that "blessed and glorious appearing", I wish, by God's help, to direct all who read this volume.*

In his sermon, 'What time is it?' he gave the following exhortation:

> *Live as if you thought Christ might come at any time. Do everything as if you did it for the last time. Say everything as if you said it for the last time. Read every chapter in the Bible as if you did not know whether you would be allowed to read it again. Pray every prayer as if you felt it might be your last opportunity...This is the way to be found ready. This is the way to turn Christ's second appearing to good account.[27]*

Albury, Powerscourt, and the Rapture

During the second quarter of the nineteenth century a number of Evangelicals came together to discuss Biblical prophecy, at a time when 'the majority of what was called the Religious World disbelieved that the Jews were to be restored to their own land, and that the Lord Jesus Christ was to return and reign in person on this earth.'[28] One of the most important venues for such gatherings was Albury Park in Surrey, the home of the wealthy landowner and Member of Parliament, Henry Drummond. The first of five annual conferences at Albury Park was inaugurated in November 1826. Those invited included Hugh McNeile, Charles Hawtrey, Edward Irving, William Cuninghame, James Haldane Stewart,

---

[27] J.C. Ryle, *Are You Ready for the End of Time?* (Fearn: Christian Focus Publications, 2001), 112, 11, 80.
[28] Henry Drummond, *Narrative of the Circumstances which led to the setting up of the Church of Christ at Albury* (1834), 7.

Spencer Perceval (Jr.), Alexander Haldane, and William 'Millennial' Marsh.

No sooner had the Albury meetings concluded than another series of prophecy conferences commenced, this time at the home of Lady Theodosia Powerscourt near Dublin. Lady Powerscourt had herself attended the inaugural Albury conference in 1826. On 4 October 1831, a number of invited clergymen and lay people, who were 'distressed at the condition of the Church ... and ... convinced that the hope of Christ's return should figure more prominently in the thinking of Christians',[29] assembled at Powerscourt House. The question of Israel again occupied much of their discussion. Among those who met at Powerscourt were some of the pioneers of the emerging Plymouth Brethren movement, including Benjamin Wills Newton, George Müller, and John Nelson Darby.

The Eye of the Believer

John Nelson Darby (1800-1882) was the London-born son of an English merchant, the godson of Admiral Horatio Lord Nelson, a Classics graduate of Trinity College, Dublin, a trained barrister, a one-time curate and priest in the Church of Ireland, and the principal architect of Plymouth Brethrenism. His legacy, though largely misunderstood and misrepresented by historians and churchmen to this day, is considerable, and is based on his unwavering devotion to Christ, his adherence to the authority of God's Word, his literal interpretation of the Scriptures, his *futurist* approach to prophecy, and his understanding of the distinction between Israel and the Church, all of which today underpin Dispensationalism and Christian Zionism.[30]

---

[29] Harold H. Rowdon, *The Origins of the Brethren 1825-1850* (London: Pickering & Inglis, 1967), 2.

[30] This is the principal thesis of my book, *For Zion's Sake: Christian Zionism and the Role of John Nelson Darby* (Milton Keynes: Paternoster, 2007).

In stark contrast to the *historicist* school of Biblical interpretation, which associates of Albury Park and the LSPCJ subscribed to, Darby maintained that apocalyptic events recorded in the book of Revelation related to a *future* period of time, and were not to be viewed retrospectively. Accordingly, the prophetic 'days', 'weeks', 'months', and 'years' of Daniel and Revelation were to be interpreted in their plain, literal, natural, and common sense, and not symbolically, as *historicists* had done since the time of the Protestant Reformation. Darby's futurist approach enabled him to successfully challenge and overturn the historicist school, which, for all its achievements in awakening the Church to the importance of Israel and the centrality of Christ's return, had failed to properly distinguish between the *earthly* inheritance of Israel (to be realised *after* the Great Tribulation) and the *heavenly* inheritance of the Church (to be realised *before* the Great Tribulation). The historicist school inevitably fell into disrepute because of its propensity to date-set not only the return of the Jews to the Land, but also, more disturbingly, the return of Jesus to Jerusalem.

In 1840, Darby observed with great anticipation how 'all the thoughts of the politicians of this world'[31] were beginning to focus on a land which, according to indisputable first-hand accounts, lay 'buried deep under the accumulated ruins of centuries.'[32] Although the Jewish people had been forcibly expelled from their land during the Roman occupation, they had remained 'ever and unchangeably loved as a people' by virtue of the *everlasting* covenant God had cut with Abraham and his descendants (Gen.

---

[31] John Nelson Darby, 'The Hopes of the Church of God, in Connection with the Destiny of the Jews and the Nations as Revealed in Prophecy (1840)', in *The Collected Writings of J.N. Darby*, ed. by William Kelly (Kingston-on-Thames: Stow Hill Bible & Tract Depot, n.d.), 2:342.
[32] Alfred Edersheim, *Sketches of Jewish Social Life in the Days of Christ* (Grand Rapids, MI: Wm. B. Eerdmans Publishing Company, 1982), 7.

17:7-8; Psa. 105:8-11). As Darby declared in his exposition of Rom. 11:25-32,

> *God's covenant to take away Israel's sins is sure. It shall be accomplished when Christ comes; for, note, the apostle speaks of Christ in Zion in a time yet to come; for God's gifts and calling suffer no change or setting aside, and Israel is His, by gift and calling, as a people...The final restoration of Israel will be on the ground of the promises made to the fathers, 'for his mercy endureth for ever.'*[33]

Although Darby's understanding of Israel was rooted in Scripture, it was his devotion to Christ and his focus on the coming of Christ *for the Church*, which enabled him to set Israel in her proper theological, and eschatological, context. As he declared in 1828, 'Let the almighty doctrine of the cross be testified to all men, and let the eye of the believer be directed to the coming of the Lord.'[34] Although men like Shaftesbury, Ryle, and the Albury Park circle all emphasised the centrality of the Second Coming, they were less clear and emphatic on the Rapture of the Church and, in particular, on its timing. This may be explained, in part, by the prevailing historicist tradition, which had misled students of Biblical prophecy for generations.

In his *Reflections upon the Prophetic Inquiry* (1829), Darby observed how, in every New Testament letter, 'the coming of the Lord Jesus is...made the prominent object of the faith and hope of believers'.[35] He drew particular inspiration from the Thessalonians, who had turned to God from idols 'to wait for His Son from heaven' (1 Thess. 1:10). The problem in the Church of

---

[33] Darby, 'Exposition of the Epistle to the Romans' (1871), in Kelly (ed.), *Collected Writings*, 26:186.
[34] Darby, 'Considerations on the Nature and Unity of the Church of Christ' (1828), in Kelly (ed.), *Collected Writings*, 1:30.
[35] Darby, 'Reflections upon the Prophetic Inquiry and the Views advanced in it (1829)', in Kelly (ed.), *Collected Writings*, 2:25.

his day was not so much 'the denial of the Lord's coming', but 'the loss of the sense and present expectation of it.'[36] The teaching that Jesus could not come for His Bride until certain prophetic events had taken place had forced the Church into prophecies relating to the time of *Jacob's* trouble (Jer. 30:7; Dan. 12:1; Matt. 24:21). As a consequence, the Rapture of the Church had been set back by at least seven years. Darby's response was unequivocal:

> *The Lord considers it important that the saints should be always expecting [His return] as a present thing, and wishing for it as a present thing...And, indeed, were I to adopt the system proposed to me, I should not expect the Lord at all until a time when I was able to fix the day of His appearing...I say fix the day, for I cannot expect His coming until the abomination of desolation is set up at Jerusalem, and then I can say, Now in twelve hundred and sixty days the Lord will be here. And this fixing by signs and dates, I am told, is the sober way of waiting. But it is quite clear that it is contrary to the way the Lord Himself has taught me to expect Him. It is clear that, if these signs are to be expected for the church, I have nothing to expect till they are fulfilled. I may expect them, and have my mind fixed on them, but not on Christ's coming. And, when one particular one happens, I can name to a day His coming. This is not what Christ has taught me, and therefore I do not receive it.[37]*

The impact of Darby's re-statement and clarification of the doctrine of the Second Coming, with the inclusion of the 'precious truth'[38] of the Rapture as the first *stage* of Christ's return, was felt

---

[36] Darby, 'The Rapture of the Saints and the Character of the Jewish Remnant', in Kelly (ed.), *Collected Writings*, 11:156.
[37] Darby, 'A Few Brief Remarks on "A Letter on Revelation 12"', in Kelly (ed.), *Collected Writings*, 11:25-27.
[38] H.A. Ironside, *A Historical Sketch of the Brethren Movement* (Neptune, NJ: Loizeaux Brothers, 1985), 23.

not only in Britain but also across North America, where a new generation of believers took up Darby's mantle.

A Prophetic Witness in Britain

Upon receiving news of the Balfour Declaration in November 1917, one of the country's most respected preachers, F.B. Meyer (1847-1929), invited a number of his fellow Christian leaders to a prayer breakfast in London. The purpose was to consider how the wider Church could be alerted to the significance of this historic development. A seven-point manifesto was subsequently drawn up and published just six days after Balfour's letter was issued. Entitled, 'The Significance of the Hour', points 1-4 of the manifesto read as follows:

> *1. That the signs of the times point towards the close of the Times of the Gentiles.*
> *2. That the return of our Lord may be expected at any moment when He will be manifested as evidently as to His disciples on the evening of His resurrection.*
> *3. That the completed church will be translated to meet the Lord in the air, and to be forever with the Lord.*
> *4. That Israel will be restored to their own land in unbelief, and afterwards converted by the manifestation of Christ as their Messiah.*

Darby's legacy can clearly be seen, even if it was not explicitly acknowledged. The manifesto was released to the national press, and public meetings were planned by F.B. Meyer and his associates, to be held on 13 December 1917 at the Queen's Hall in London.[39] In his address that day, F.S. Webster spoke of the joy felt by all speakers over news of Allenby's liberation of Jerusalem, which had been secured just four days earlier. However, Webster's

---

[39] Colin Le Noury, *In the Steps of F.B. Meyer: 90 Years of Prophetic Witness* (Belfast: Ambassador Productions, 2008), 19-20.

joy for Israel was tempered with sadness over the spiritual state of the Church. As he explained,

> The chief fault of Christians today is that they do not make enough of the Lord Jesus Christ...It is good and right to preach Christ incarnate, Christ crucified, Christ risen, Christ ascended, but if we would be true to the Scripture we must add one more note – Christ returning, Christ coming again...Now the danger of the present day...is this, that just because the Lord delayeth His coming...people have let slip the blessed hope of His coming again...If we really belong to Him, if we really believe in Him, we shall love His appearing, we shall long for His coming again.[40]

The Advent Testimony Movement was launched shortly after. Later renamed the Advent Testimony and Preparation Movement, it continues to proclaim the any-moment coming of Christ under the name Prophetic Witness Movement International. Among those who emerged as its early leaders and speakers were General Sir William Dobbie, Bishop Handley Moule, Revd W. Graham Scroggie, and Dr Frederick Tatford, all of whom 'kept continual watch on happenings in the Middle East, in the firm belief that the nation of Israel would one day be re-established'[41] and that Christ would soon appear.

An American Awakening
In the years preceding the American Civil War (1861-1865), a number of books were published which helped trigger a premillennial revival in the largely postmillennial American Church. Such books included Edward Winthrop's *Lectures on the Second Advent* (1843), Jacob Janeway's *Hope for the Jews* (1853),

---

[40] *Advent Testimony Addresses delivered at the Meetings at Queen's Hall, London, W.C., December 13th, 1917* (London: Chas. J. Thynne, 1918), 84-88.
[41] Le Noury, *In the Steps of F.B. Meyer*, p. 85.

John Cumming's *Signs of the Times* (1854), and Joseph Seiss's *The Last Times* (1856). However, it was the visit of John Nelson Darby to the United States in 1862 which proved to be of greater significance.

Between 1862 and 1877, Darby crossed the continent of North America seven times, travelling 'on the skirts of the [American Civil] war' in 1863. He recalled in a letter from Toronto that year that he had travelled 'about 2,000 miles in the last four weeks'.[42] Wherever he went his mission remained the same, namely 'to present Christ and the truth, accomplished salvation, and His coming.'[43] Chicago pastor and evangelist, Dwight L. Moody (1837-1899), was among the many Church leaders who were inspired by Darby's devotion to Scripture, and his 'uncompromising belief in the imminent, bodily, and premillennial return of the Lord Jesus Christ'.[44] Another was James Hall Brookes (1830-1897), who heard Darby speak in St. Louis 'with great pleasure and profit'.[45] Brookes was the driving force behind the Bible and Prophecy Conference Movement, which propagated and popularised the dispensationalist message.[46] According to C. Norman Kraus, 'there can be little room for doubt that Darby and other early Plymouth Brethren preachers gave direct stimulus and at least indirect guidance to the movement.'[47] In his final letter from America, written in June 1877, Darby made the following observation: 'The truth is spreading...For some time

---

[42] Darby, 'Letter to Mr Pollock (Toronto, 27 May 1863)', in J.N. Darby, *Letters of J.N.D.* (Kingston-on-Thames: Stow Hill Bible & Tract Depot, n.d.), 1:351-352.

[43] Darby, 'Letter to G. Biava (New York, 1873)', in Darby, *Letters of J.N.D.*, 2:212.

[44] Lyle W. Dorsett, *A Passion for Souls: The Life of D.L. Moody* (Chicago, IL: Moody Publishers, 1997), 136.

[45] Quoted in R.A. Huebner, *Elements of Dispensational Truth: Vol. I*, 2nd edn (Morganville, NJ: Present Truth Publishers, 1998), 20.

[46] See Wilkinson, *For Zion's Sake*, 247-251.

[47] C. Norman Kraus, *Dispensationalism in America* (Richmond, VA: John Knox Press, 1958), 79.

the coming of the Lord has wrought in souls far and wide, and the doctrine is spreading wonderfully.'[48]

Conclusion

Shortly after Darby's death on 29 April 1882, the following tribute appeared in *The Christian Commonwealth*:

> *There has recently passed away one of the most remarkable servants of Christ that this country has produced. We refer to Mr. John Nelson Darby...It would have been too much to expect that any lengthened notice of this remarkable man should have a place in the daily papers, or that he should find a sepulchre amongst the great men of our national history. Nevertheless, it is true to say that the movement of which he was, at once, one of the principal leaders, was most distinguished for vitality, force, and widespread influence.*

At Darby's funeral, a member of the Brethren read Jn. 14:1-3 and 1 Thess. 4:15-18, and spoke of the 'precious' and 'distinctive truths' concerning the 'coming of the Lord to take His Church', which had become 'familiar to thousands, and perhaps tens of thousands in the Church of God.' He proceeded to speak of 'the great goodness of our God and Father in using our beloved departed brother as His vessel to restore these and other blessed truths to the Church', and prayed that 'the coming of the Lord, as the *immediate* hope of believers...might more than ever be a living and operative truth in our souls.'[49]

One man who was deeply indebted to John Nelson Darby was William Blackstone, whose petition influenced Woodrow Wilson at such a crucial moment in history. In his book, *Jesus is Coming*, Blackstone included several stanzas from a hymn penned

---

[48] Darby, 'Letter to Mr. Brockhaus (7 June 1877)', in Darby, *Letters of J.N.D.*, 2:395.

[49] *The Last Days of J.N.D. (John Nelson Darby) From March 3rd to April 29th, 1882, With Portrait*, 2nd edn (Christchurch: N.C.M. Turner, 1925), 26, 22-23.

by Hannah K. Burlingham, who was a member of the Plymouth Brethren. Entitled, 'I'm Waiting For Thee, Lord', the hymn was included by the Brethren in their *Hymns and Spiritual Songs for the Little Flock*, and inspired Darby to write his own version, 'The Soul's Desire' (1881), shortly before his death. Blackstone included Burlingham's hymn to highlight not only the doctrine of Christ's *any-moment* return, but also the longing for His return which Christ looks for in the heart of every believer. The opening verse of the hymn reads as follows:

> *I'm waiting for Thee, Lord,*
> *Thy beauty to see, Lord,*
> *I'm waiting for Thee,*
> *For Thy coming again.*
> *Thou'rt gone over there, Lord,*
> *A place to prepare, Lord,*
> *Thy home I shall share*
> *At Thy coming again.*[50]

To men like Darby and Blackstone, the Second Coming was far more than a doctrine to be preached and expounded; it was a blessed hope that needed to burn brightly in the heart of every believer, as it had once done in the heart of the Apostle Paul and the early Church (2 Tim. 4:8). The return of the Jewish people to their homeland, after nearly two millennia in exile, not only vindicated nineteenth-century Evangelicals who faithfully proclaimed that God had 'by no means' rejected or replaced His people Israel (Rom. 11:1), but convinced many that Christ's return was near. Following the liberation of Jerusalem on 9 December 1917, Sir Robert Anderson (1841-1918), the Assistant Commissioner at Scotland Yard for thirteen years, a member of the Plymouth Brethren, a friend of John Nelson Darby, and an

---

[50] Blackstone, *Jesus is Coming*, p. 215; *cf.* J.N. Darby, *Spiritual Songs* (Lancing: Kingston Bible Trust, 1974), 71.

associate of the Advent Testimony Movement, expressed his personal conviction that Allenby's triumph

> *gives hope that we are nearing the age in which they [the Jews] will be restored to favour, and therefore that the Lord's coming for us [the Church], which must precede that restoration, may be close at hand.*[51]

Anderson's conviction is conspicuous by its absence in what we may loosely term 'the pro-Israel Church' today, where the priority for many believers lies in expressing solidarity with the Jewish people and the Jewish State, rather than in exclaiming the midnight cry, 'Behold, the Bridegroom!' (Matt. 25:6). The Church in this country appears to have forsaken not only the prophetic witness of many of its Evangelical forebears, but her first love (Rev. 2:4). In *Jesus is Coming*, William Blackstone included the following letter, which had been sent to him by a 'dear brother' in Christ. May it serve to stir the hearts of many in the Church today, so that all true believers might look, with eager longing and expectation, for the coming of the Heavenly Bridegroom:

> *I find so many who are willing to receive the truth of the Second Coming, but it is generally those who are passing through affliction, or those living very near the Lord. Those who are enjoying the well watered plains of this world, seem to care very little about seeing the Owner of the Estate. But He will come. Hallelujah! He will come. Yes! He is coming. The bride who knows the Bridegroom, and is true, says, He is coming. 'Come Lord Jesus,' Come! Come!! Come!!! Come!!!! A poor cursed earth (Rom. 8:19-22) groans out Come! Thank heaven, He speaks: 'SURELY I COME QUICKLY.' Rev. 22:20.*[52]

---

[51] Sir Robert Anderson, *Unfulfilled Prophecy; and The Hope of the Church*, 2nd edn (London: James Nisbet & Co. Ltd., 1918), vii.
[52] Blackstone, *Jesus is Coming*, 215.

CHAPTER 7

Faith and Politics in the Holy Land Today[1]

Calvin L. Smith

The past fifteen years or so has witnessed considerable academic Evangelical interest in the Arab-Israeli conflict. I believe there are several reasons for this. First, a changing Arab-Israeli narrative in recent decades has caught the world's (and Evangelicals') attention. Despite being rejected by the extreme left as an imperialist ideology, between the end of the Second World War and the Six Day War in 1967 Zionism and the fledgling state of Israel enjoyed some (if somewhat begrudging) support in the West. The horrors of the Holocaust clearly contributed to this. Also, early Zionism was essentially collectivist (the communal kibbutz system being a prime example), thus garnering respect from some on the moderate left. Moreover, Israel's survival against the odds while surrounded by enemies seeking her annihilation won her much admiration.

Yet Israel's nation-building success, the creation of a strong economy (compared with poorer surrounding Arab countries), and growing military prowess, have arguably resulted in the Zionist narrative undergoing considerable change in recent years, from a small but plucky pioneer movement to that of regional superpower. Also, from 1987 ongoing Palestinian *intifada* has contributed to raising the profile of the conflict considerably, so that the David versus Goliath narrative has, in much of the world's

---

[1] This is a revised version of a paper delivered to the joint Ethics and Social Theology with Religion, Culture and Communication study groups, Tyndale Fellowship conference, Cambridge, 9 July 2008. The complete research is contracted for publication with Paternoster in 2010 in a book entitled *Sons of Abraham: The Politics of Christian Faith in the Holy Land.*

eyes, become inverted. Meanwhile, the rise of Islamism, the events of 9/11, neoconservatism under a Bush administration, American and British adventurism in Iraq, and anti-Americanism (a nation of which Israel is regarded as a client) have all contributed to how the Middle East conflict is perceived globally.

All this comes as Evangelicals are moving beyond political declarations on a handful of moral issues (for example, abortion and homosexuality) to engage with the political sphere in a wider-ranging manner.[2] Evangelical politics has also witnessed the rise of a vocal Evangelical Left, which tends to be critical of Israel and Christian Zionism. Meanwhile, anti-Israel rhetoric by some Palestinian Christian leaders during the *intifada* period (reasons for this are discussed later) has also contributed to raising the profile of the Arab-Israeli conflict in Evangelical circles.

At the same time, Anglican calls for disinvestment of their financial portfolio from Israel, as well as a shift away from post-Holocaust theology, which emerged as a result of considerable soul-searching by Europe's historic denominations in the wake of the Holocaust, feed into the current debate. The result has been the emergence of a Christian Zionist counterpart, so-called Christian Palestinianism[3]. Support for either position, together with the perennial theological issue of what constitutes 'Israel', has resulted in a flurry of books in recent years within Evangelical academic circles, all contributing to a debate which is becoming increasingly intense, polarised, and bitter.

To date, Christian responses to Israel have tended to revolve around the study of texts such as Romans 9-11,[4] or biblical

---

[2] For a brief discussion, see my `Editorial: The De-privatisation of Faith and Evangelicals in the Public Square', *Evangelical Review of Society and Politics* 1.1 (February 2007), 1-20.

[3] This term appears in Paul Wilkinson's *For Zion's Sake: Christian Zionism and the Role of John Nelson Darby* (Milton Keynes: Paternoster, 2007), and was presumably coined by him.

[4] A useful book which identifies and comments on the key prooftexts cited by either side is *Ronald Diprose, Israel and the Church: The*

theology themes such as the land, justice, and treatment of the alien as set out in the Torah. In this book Stephen Vantassel offers an eloquent treatment of the land, while in Chapter 2 I explore the issue of the alien before moving on to another theme, the house of Israel (that is, ethnic Jews as the people of God). By focusing on the people *rather* than the land, I do not automatically preclude on theological grounds the principle of giving up at least some land for peace (depending on which land and if political circumstances ever permit). I am not convinced, for example, Ariel Sharon's disengagement from Gaza was unjustifiable for strictly theological reasons. After all, the land of the Philistines did not belong to biblical Israel. Now there are some who will cite Israel's right to the Gaza strip (the land of the Philistines) on the basis of Obadiah 19. But Obadiah 19 is eschatological in context (the reference to the 'day of the Lord' in verse 15 suggests this, cf. Joel 1:15, 2:1, 11, 31, 3:14). If, then, Obadiah 19 is eschatological its ultimate fulfilment (when it finally takes place) is final and irreversible, and therefore *no one* – whether Ariel Sharon or anyone else – can reverse or influence the divine plan. God's eternal plan will be accomplished no matter what. However, let me state clearly and categorically that, from a political perspective, Sharon's withdrawal from Gaza has proved a strategic disaster. In all honesty, I do not see a lasting peace with Islamist Hamas, whose long-term strategy is ultimately the destruction of the Jewish state. It is, after all, the basis of their charter, which is why they will only ever contemplate a temporary truce, never a permanent ceasefire. For them, establishing pre-1967 borders is simply part of a piecemeal strategy aimed at turning the clock back to *before* 1948. So politically, giving up land for peace is presently unworkable.

Leaving aside the various hermeneutical, biblical theology and religio-political treatments of the Israel issue, in this chapter I want to look at Israel from a somewhat different perspective.

Origins and Effects of Replacement Theology (Waynesboro, GA: Authentic Media, 2004).

Several supercessionists and Palestinian church leaders accuse the Jewish state of adopting policies which oppress Arab Christians, and also maintain that Arab Christians reject Israel theologically as God's chosen people. As a regular visitor and study trip leader to Israel I am in a good position to do fieldwork, and so I decided to research the extent to which the evidence on the ground bears out this view. But I also decided to explore the nature of relations between Jewish believers in Jesus and the Israel state. A study of Christian-state relations in the Holy Land provides a useful contribution to the debate on how we as Christians should respond to the modern state of Israel and the current Middle East conflict. This chapter, then, is based on ongoing fieldwork, interviews and research in both Israel and the Palestinian Territories. While not yet complete, the emerging narrative contradicts blanket claims by pro-Palestinian Christians that Israel systematically oppresses its Arab Christian population. But it also rejects some Christian Zionists' claims that Christians in the Holy Land enjoy full protection by the Israeli authorities.

ARAB CHRISTIAN RELATIONS WITH THE STATE OF ISRAEL

Blanket claims that all Palestinian Christians are critical of Israel and reject her theologically are unsophisticated. The views of organisations such as Sabeel, an ecumenical body which espouses Palestinian liberation theology (even coming close to condoning suicide bombings on the basis of Samson's last act in the temple of Dagon, though claiming not to condone such actions)[5] are not embraced by all Arab Christians in the Holy Land. Neither do all Arab Christians blame Israel for their genuinely difficult situation.

---

[5] Naim Ateek, Suicide Bombers: What is Theologically and Morally Wrong With Suicide Bombings? A Palestinian Christian Perspective' in *Cornerstone* 25 (Summer 2002). This was originally posted on Sabeel's website at www.sabeel.org/old/news/cstone25/suicidebombers.htm (accessed 5 May 2007), but appears since to have been removed.

First, we must differentiate between Arab Christian leaders of the historic denominations and the grassroots laity. The former often express anti-Israel rhetoric, which some Arab Christians told me is a survival strategy by church leaders who recognise the peace process' focus on a two-state solution means one day they will come under the control of the Palestinian Authority. As such, these church leaders feel the need to establish their Palestinian nationalist credentials now if they and their congregations are to survive in the future. After all, Arab Christianity already faces considerable challenges as a religious minority within the Territories. Moreover, a recent piece of research details how an historically secular Palestinian population has swung strongly towards militant Islamism in the past fifteen years or so.[6] Another study details how Muslim Israeli Arabs have captured political control of Nazareth for the past two decades, where Christians were formerly in the majority, passing local laws which have had a detrimental effect on Arab Christianity resulting in many Christians leaving Nazareth.[7] The emergence of Palestinian Islamism makes the future of Arab Christianity (whether historic denominations or non-denominational) in a future Palestinian state even more precarious, which helps to explain why some historic church leaders criticise Israel so vociferously. I do not suggest this is their only motive, and we shall have more to say about this later. But such anti-Israel rhetoric must be understood within its endogenous context.

This view by church leaders is echoed by some grassroots Arab Christians, but certainly not all (or even the majority). Many are not convinced Israel is the cause of all Arab Christianity's problems. For example, a Catholic Jerusalemite currently researching Arab Christianity for a Ph.D. with a European

---

[6] See Loren. D. Lybarger, *Identity and Religion in Palestine: The Struggle Between Islamism and Secularism in the Occupied Territories* (Princeton University Press, 2007).

[7] Raphael Israeli, *Green Crescent Over Nazareth: The Displacement of Christians by Muslims in the Holy Land* (London: Frank Cass, 2002).

university, told me how many Arab lay Christians were disillusioned with their church leaders' failure to improve the situation of a Christian minority which feels increasingly under siege from economic difficulties, Islamic encroachment and a diminishing Christian population through emigration.[8] These are real problems, he explained, which demand action by church leaders. But instead all the mainstream church leaders do is blame everything on the Israeli occupation, a convenient scapegoat which excuses their own leadership failures. It is significant that this individual is a Palestinian nationalist who has little love for Israel. Yet his research and analysis lead him to conclude that Arab Christianity's problems cannot all be laid at Israel's feet. Ineffective church leadership within some of the historic denominations, which is at odds with its grassroots, is at least partly to blame.

Various lay Christians echoed similar views, and a distinct difference of opinion emerged between Arab Christian leaders and grassroots within historic denominations concerning their perception of Israel. Some lay Christians clearly had no love for Israel (though most claimed to get on quite well with their Jewish neighbours), but few expressed the strong anti-Israeli rhetoric of their high-profile leaders speaking to a Western audience. Several Christians from historic denominations were even quite generous towards the Israeli state and said they actually *preferred* Israeli rule to the prospect of coming under the Palestinian Authority. Joseph, an Orthodox Jerusalemite businessman, explained how he genuinely liked much about the Jewish state.[9] Moreover, as an Arab Christian he said he far preferred being with Jews than Arab Muslims, with whom he and other Arab Christians he knew had faced various problems. He explained how a Muslim business rival kept making problems for him, as well as continuously

---

[8] Interview, East Jerusalem, 4 February 2008. Given the difficulties of speaking out candidly in such a tense environment, he asked for me not to publish his identity.
[9] Conversation, Jerusalem's Old City, 5 February 2008.

suggest he should emigrate, as so many other Arab Christians were doing. This issue of Islam came up frequently during the various interviews, with many Christians expressing concern about their faith's existence as a diminishing minority under the Palestinian Authority, particularly with a shift towards Islamism among parts of the Palestinian population.

Aside from the differences of opinion between Arab Christian leaders and laity, it is also important to differentiate between mainstream historic denominations (for example, Lutheran, Anglican) and Evangelicals. The latter consists of both supercessionists and those who believe the Jews remain in some sense God's chosen people. Some even appreciate and talk openly about the Jewish root of their faith. In Haifa, there is an Arab pastor who leads a Messianic congregation.[10] Others speak out against replacement theology. For example, in Jerusalem I was introduced to a Pentecostal Arab former pastor who stated categorically the land belonged to the Jews and the Muslims had no right to it whatsoever.[11] I also met an Arab pastor near the West Bank who took a particularly strong Dispensationalist line, explaining how in the last days the land would be inhabited by Jews only, while God's covenant with the Arabs guaranteed them inheritances of territory alongside a Greater Israel.[12] Leaving aside his theology and links with American groups, such views fly in the face of claims that Arab Christians are all supercessionists. I do not want to give the impression all Arab Christians monolithically view Israel positively. In fact, my point is quite the opposite: Arab Christian perceptions of Israel are *far* from homogenous. Many dislike Israel, yet others consider Israeli rule far more preferable to a future Palestinian authority. Some, like Samir, an Evangelical from Jerusalem, believe in a future divine plan for the Jews but

---

[10] For details see Kai Kjær-Hansen and Bodil F. Skjøtt, *Facts and Myths About the Messianic Congregations in Israel* (Jerusalem: United Christian Council in Israel and the Caspari Center, 1999),163-7.

[11] Interview, Jerusalem's Old City, 2 February 2008.

[12] Interview, 5 February 2008.

believes the Israeli occupation, together with economic problems, are partly to blame for the exodus of Christians.[13] The point I am simply making is that Arab Christianity's perceptions of Israel, both politically and theologically, are not, as some anti-Israel Evangelical writers would have us believe, united in their hatred of the Israeli state, or that all Arab Christians in the Holy Land are supercessionists.

As well as differentiating between leaders and laity, historic and Evangelical Christianity, and also the different theological and political views within Evangelicalism vis-à-vis Israel, we must also take into account differing geographical experiences of Arab Christianity. Jerusalem is very different from the West Bank. In the Jewish capital Christian Arabs are a double minority, squeezed between two far larger faiths (Judaism and Islam). Yet all three faiths do manage to get on, though tensions arise from time to time. (Samir explained how Jerusalem tends to be better for Christians, though the Danish cartoon protests had caused Christian-Muslim relations to deteriorate considerably in the city).[14] In the West Bank, where Islam is dominant, Christians experience various problems. For example, Joseph explained how Muslims regarded Christian girls who did not wear a headscarf as promiscuous and an easy target.[15] A report in the *Jerusalem Post* echoed how Jerusalemite Christian girls were treated inappropriately by Muslim young men.[16] I came across various other stories of difficulties West Bank Christians faced, mainly fairly minor issues but which together have an accumulative effect. Moreover, there is a difference between the West Bank and Gaza, where Christianity represents a tiny minority, and where there have been several high-profile cases of Christian oppression,

---

[13] Conversation, Jerusalem's Old City, 5 February 2008.
[14] Ibid.
[15] Conversation with Joseph, op. cit.
[16] David Smith, `Christians Anonymous', *In Jerusalem* (a *Jerusalem Post* weekend supplement), 1 February 2008, 10-13.

including the murder of a prominent Christian leader, since Hamas took over.

What of Israeli perceptions and treatment of Arab Christians? Despite many Arab Christians' preference for Israeli rule, several said they were regarded with suspicion by the Israeli authorities in much the same way as Muslim Arabs. Joseph, who expressed some particularly strong pro-Israel comments, was nonetheless frustrated that the authorities often do not differentiate between Arab Christians such as himself, who likes Israel, and some of the very Arab Muslims he feels are causing problems for him and his fellow Christians.[17] Others echoed similar views. Arguably, Israel has reason to be suspicious of some Israeli Arabs, who have been implicated in terrorist plots, while several of their MKs (Knesset Members) have fraternised with Israel's enemies. Yet not all Israeli Arabs are enemies of the state. For example, a sizeable number want to take up a new form of Arab national service (which Arab Israeli leaders have rejected).[18] Hence, many Arab Israelis (including Arab Christians) are frustrated that they are all regarded with such suspicion by the Israelis.

Moreover, Israeli security policies have had an economic bearing on parts of the Arab Christian population, for example, in Bethlehem (though tourism is well up on previous years). Arab Christians are leaving Bethlehem in large numbers, and clearly the security fence/wall and its economic effects on tourism have at least partially contributed to this emigration.

Yet it should be noted that Israeli security policy is not the only factor at work which indirectly affects Arab Christian wellbeing. One Palestinian businessman explained how, besides the security fence and long IDF checkpoints, poor Palestinian Authority administration and a monopoly of tourism by a handful of Arab families, or clans, were all contributing to Bethlehem's

---

[17] Conversation with Joseph, op. cit.
[18] Leslie Susser, `National Service Seeks Arab Volunteers', *The Jerusalem Report* (28 April 2008), 12-16.

economic woes.[19] It is also important to move beyond the simplistic statement that Bethlehem's Christian population has been falling steadily since the state of Israel was founded in 1948. Indeed, in 1948 some 85% of Bethlehem's population was Christian, while today it is around 12%.[20] Thus, it is easy to extrapolate from these statistics that the founding of Israel is somehow responsible for the demise of Arab Christianity in Bethlehem. But while this may be so, there is much more to this story. Consider how the Christian population in the city in 1967 was 42.6%.[21] This means it halved between 1948 and 1967, when Bethlehem was *not* under Israeli control. Moreover, the exodus of Christians has *increased* since the First Intifada.

Clearly, then, the economic situation is a major part of the problem, but anti-Christian Muslim feelings also contribute to Christianity's demise. During a visit there for several days, Archbishop of Canterbury Rowan Williams observed that as well as life made intolerable by the security fence, there were 'some signs of disturbing anti-Christian feelings among parts of the Muslim population'. One Baptist minister claimed his church in Bethlehem had been attacked with Molotov cocktails 14 times in recent times.[22] Catholic Palestinian landowner in Bethlehem Jiryas Handal had land expropriated by Israel to build a neighbourhood on land annexed in 1967. But he also had land taken by his Muslim neighbours. The Palestinian authorities promised to intervene repeatedly, but nothing ever happened and the land was never returned.[23] So clearly there are various factors at work which explain why Arab Christians are emigrating from the Holy Land. By constantly focusing on Israeli aggression and occupation

---

[19] Jorg Luyken, `Room at the Inn?' *International Jerusalem Post* 2460 (2007), 24-5.

[20] Lela Gilbert, `Bethlehem Beyond the Christmas Calm', *International Jerusalem Post* 2461 (2007), 18-19.

[21] Barak Barfi, 'Land Grab in Bethlehem', *The Jerusalem Report* (7 January 2008), 24-6.

[22] Lela Gilbert, op. cit.

[23] Barak Barfi, op. cit.

and nothing else, Christian `Palestinianists' are ignoring other issues faced by Arab Christians which must be dealt with if the haemorrhage of Christians from the land is to be stopped.

MESSIANIC CHRISTIAN RELATIONS AND THE STATE OF ISRAEL

If the perceptions and experiences of Arab Christians vis-à-vis Israel have been generalised and presented as homogenous, the nature and extent of Messianic Christian-Israeli state relations have been all but ignored. The number of Jewish Christians is very small, somewhere between 10,000 and 15,000 (there are probably another 15,000 to 20,000 Christians who entered Israel under the right of return as relatives of Russian Jews).[24] Being such a small number, together with the view prevalent among Haredi (or Ultra-Orthodox) Jews that to become a Christian means ceasing to be a Jew, has caused considerable problems for Israel's Messianic believers. Like their Arab Christian counterparts in predominantly Muslim areas, they feel under siege from the dominant religious faith. To what extent have their relations with the state exacerbated this situation?

Messianic Jews supposedly enjoy full religious freedom and legal protection of their rights. Moreover, the Israeli state and constitution is secular, as are many of its politicians, so in theory Jewish Christians are treated no differently from any other faith. But Israel is currently witnessing not only a growing Ultra-Orthodox population, but also one which is growing in political power. With every visit to Israel one is struck by an increasingly polarised society divided along religious-secular lines. Moreover,

---

[24] There are various statistical analyses of Jewish Christianity in Israel, but the most detailed work has been carried out by the Caspari Center, Jerusalem. A useful book on the nature and extent of Messianic congregations is the important survey by Kai Kjaer-Hansen and Bodil F. Skjott, *Facts and Myths* (op. cit.). Unfortunately, this work is now a decade old.

Ultra-Orthodox Jews are increasingly involved in Israeli politics, forming their own parties and getting laws passed which impact not only their supporters, but which also have a bearing on non-religious Jews (for example, rules on Shabbat, smoking during Passover/hametz, and so on).

Not all Ultra-Orthodox Jews are Zionist, but at this particular moment in time the majority are, refusing to sanction calls to give away parts of Jerusalem to a Palestinian authority. Meanwhile, settler activity as a whole is driven by Jewish Ultra-Orthodox theology. (In an allusion to the rock group Guns and Roses, a T-shirt is available for sale in Jerusalem showing a picture of an Ultra-Orthodox face, complete with *peyot* (hair locks) above an image of two tablets of stone (the Decalogue) next to a machine gun. Underneath is the caption: *Guns and Moses.*)

The Ultra-Orthodox have formed their own political parties, the best-known and most powerful being Shas, a Sephardic party. Another is United Torah Judaism, which is Ashkenazi. Because of the nature of Israeli politics, which relies on coalition governments, such parties often punch far above their weight and their power is disproportionate to their size. Within Ehud Olmert's government Shas was an important coalition party, holding a sizeable percentage of Knesset seats.[25] When Shas considered leaving the government, Olmert's position became precarious.[26] Moreover, during the Olmert administration Shas practiced its own foreign policy agenda, blatantly seeking to set up channels of communication with Hamas (though not for a lasting peace settlement; a ceasefire is their preferred option, which would save Jewish lives without actually having to give up land).[27] Such communication went totally against the Olmert government policy of not speaking with the Islamist organisation, yet Shas remained

---

[25] For a discussion of Shas' political power, see Leslie Susser, `Shas Flexes Its Muscles' in *The Jerusalem Report* (26 May 2008), 10-13.
[26] Gil Hoffman, `Shas leader Eli Yishai: I'm ready to leave government tomorrow' in *International Jerusalem Post* 2483 (6-12 June 2008), 6.
[27] See Leslie Susser, op. cit.

in government and communicated with Hamas anyway, demonstrating just how weak and confident Olmert and Shas were respectively.

Importantly, coalition support from Shas and other Orthodox parties – arguably the kingmakers of Israeli politics – comes at a price, mainly in the form of getting their religious policies on the statute books. This has occurred at a piecemeal pace, but the Ultra-Orthodox impact on a secular Israel has been steady. The movement has a powerful voice in determining who can make *aliya* (immigration to Israel), enjoys important positions in the state bureaucracy, and is passing laws which make life increasingly difficult for Israel's Messianic Christian community, which are regarded by Orthodox Jews as traitors.

At this stage, we shall consider briefly the nature of Haredi-Messianic relations. Ultra-Orthodox Jews regard Christianity and Judaism as completely incompatible: you cannot be Jewish and a Christian. (In fact, within Jewish Christianity the same debate is taking place, with some leaders, such as Baruch Maoz arguing for a complete break with Judaism, while others, notably Mark Kinzer, calling for Messianic integration into the Jewish religious community, who should aim to win converts to Yeshua by example.)[28]

Missionary activity is despised by Orthodox Jews, who associate it with centuries of persecution and forced conversion in a Europe plagued with a history of Christian anti-Semitism. Jewish Christian congregations are deeply aware of such sensitivities, and they themselves struggle with determining the nature of their identity. For some, even to call oneself a Christian suggests no longer being Jewish, as well as causing problems within the community and making one's Christian witness that

---

[28] Both these positions can be summed up in the titles of books written by both Jewish Christian leaders: Baruch Maoz, *Judaism Is Not Jewish* (Christian Focus, 2003), and Mark. S. Kinzer, *Post-Missionary Messianic Judaism: Redefining Christian Engagement with the Jewish People* (Grand Rapids, Michigan: Brazos Press, 2005).

much more difficult. Meanwhile, links with exogenous (external) Gentile Christian organisations fuels Ultra-Orthodox claims that Messianic groups are engaging in missionary activity to convert Jews to Christianity. All this is a real problem for Messianic Jews, but especially so in Israel, where the powerful Ultra-Orthodox community despises them. Arguably, much of this is also because the Haredim feel threatened by Jewish believers in Jesus. There are many secret believers in Yeshua among the Ultra-Orthodox (so-called Nicodemus Christians), and Ultra-Orthodox anti-missionary activity is intense, aggressive, and sometimes violent.

Foremost among the anti-missionary organisations is an organisation called Yad L'achim. Baruch Maoz, a leading Jewish believer in Israel, says Yad L'achim receives substantial financial support from the Israeli government. They also cull information on Messianic Jews and organisations from government files.[29] Examples of anti-missionary activity aimed at Jewish Christians include graffiti, tyres being slashed, telephone threats, and arson. During visits to Jerusalem I have stayed several times at an old church near the Jaffa Gate of the Old City. One of the church trustees described how one day he caught three Ultra-Orthodox youths trying to set fire to the building. This is just one of several problems they have encountered in the past. I have also seen old Haredis walk by and curse and spit at the church. A favoured technique of Yad L'achim is to put up picture posters of local Messianic believers and organisations, including their addresses, in order to denounce them and warn the wider Jewish population off. Just recently, hundreds of New Testaments which had been given to Ethiopian Jews by Messianic Jews were publicly burned by Yeshiva students in Or Yehuda. The Deputy Mayor, a Shas politician, was eventually forced to apologise to Christians worldwide.[30]

Sometimes, Ultra-Orthodox anti-Christian activity can be violent. Cases include besieging Christians in Arad, the burning of

---

[29] As cited in Kai Kjaer-Hansen and Bodil F. Skjott, op. cit.
[30] `In Brief', *International Jerusalem Post* 2481 (23-29 May 2008), 6.

a church in Jerusalem, and a siege by over a thousand Ultra-Orthodox upon a church in Beersheva. I met with the pastor, Howard Bass, who explained how a rumour had circulated that his church was about to bring in three busloads of Jewish children to baptise them into the Christian faith (in fact, only three Israelis were to be baptised that day, all of them aged eighteen or over).[31] Proselytising minors is against the law in Israel, while such conversions have historical parallels in Europe's treatment of its Jews. And so over a thousand religious Jews descended upon the church, causing considerable damage and roughing up members of the congregation. It later transpired it had been Ultra-Orthodox anti-missionary leaders who had circulated the rumour and organised the protest. More recently, during this year's Purim festival, a bomb was sent to a Christian family, which severely injured the pastor's son when it exploded (I later interviewed the family, met the son and saw pictures of the damage to the house and injuries sustained by the son, which were horrific). This was believed to have been the work of Orthodox Jews. When interviewed by the *Jerusalem Post*, Howard Bass said anti-missionary violence has been going on for years in Israel, but nobody will take a stand and help Messianic believers.[32] Indeed, threats against Messianic believers are frequent. They are regarded as a dangerous cult and traitors, and organisations such as Jews for Jesus are brave in their Christian witness against such fierce opposition.

Meanwhile, Evangelical organisations based in Israel sometimes face great difficulty getting visas renewed for their workers, this despite their pro-Israel stance. Recently, this issue was taken up by the Knesset's cross-party *Christian Allies Caucus* (an organisation which recognises Christian support for Israel), but the matter failed to reach the upper echelons of government.[33] Messianic Jews also face problems making *aliya* (immigrating to

---

[31] Interview, Beersheva, 11 February 2008.
[32] `In Brief', *International Jerusalem Post* 2474 (2008), 8.
[33] `In Brief', *International Jerusalem Post* 2460 (2007), 9.

Israel), because rabbis play a central role in determining whether or not someone is Jewish. Also, by capturing important positions in the state bureaucracy, Ultra-Orthodox Jews make life increasingly difficult for Messianic believers.

Aside from Israeli government financing of organisations such as Yad L'achim, how else does the Israeli state have a bearing on Jewish Christianity? The authorities, particularly the police, often do not do much to help Messianic believers who experience persecution. But Baruch Maoz explained how, despite such persecution, when such matters came before the Israeli courts Christians were nearly always vindicated.[34] Thus Messianic groups have now taken to bringing Ultra-Orthodox anti-Christian harassment to the courts, even though this can take years to work its way though the legal system. For its part, the Israeli government's reliance on Ultra-Orthodox political parties means that, indirectly at least, the Israeli state is having a detrimental impact on the plight of Jewish believers in Jesus. These Jewish Christians are the descendants of the very first New Testament Church, which was Jewish, the first church in the land. Yet they face very much the same kind of religious persecution at the hand of religious Jews as described in the book of Acts.

CONCLUDING REMARKS

The main threat Christians face in the Holy Land today is more religious than strictly political. More accurately, this threat is religio-political, instigated by two rival faiths – Islam and Judaism – both of which are increasingly and militantly politically-active. Moreover, in both cases the governing authorities – Israel and the Palestinian Authority – do little to help their respective Christian communities. By doing little (likely because they do not wish to alienate their own religious blocs simply to support a tiny Christian minority), they indirectly exacerbate further the situation

---

[34] Interview with Baruch Maoz, near Tel Aviv, 11 February 2008.

faced by both Arab and Jewish Christians. Yet ironically, both Israel and the Palestinian Authority seek to project *externally* their pro-Christian credentials, recognising the wider propaganda and lobbying value of such to a Western audience regarded as Christian. Thus, Israel courts Christian Zionists, while Yasser Arafat (and more recently Mahmoud Abbas) claimed to be a defender of Christianity against Israeli aggression, choreographing media images of attendance at Christian places of worship and holy sites, such as the Church of the Nativity in Bethlehem. Hamas, too, seeks to portray itself as defender of its tiny Christian community. Yet the reality is completely at odds with such propaganda efforts, with increased violent attacks on Gazan Christians since Hamas snatched power.

How might this narrative affect how we as Western Christians view the current conflict? In the first instance, it is important to recognise just how complex the situation is and avoid making polemical pronouncements which merely echo the propaganda battle being played out in the secular sphere. Substantial nuance is required to understand the situation of Christians in the Holy Land. We need to differentiate between leaders and laity, historic and Evangelical, Jerusalem and the West Bank, West Bank and Gaza, Arab Christians and Messianic believers, the political influence and power of Christianity's two rival faiths in the region, and the pragmatic needs of two governing authorities vying for a propaganda victory in a particularly bitter regional conflict. By ignoring these complexities and blindly supporting either side we are merely contributing to the present war of words.

Furthermore, to pro-Palestinian Christians I would ask: Why it is that many Arab Christians do not demonise Israel as they do? Very many Arab Christians actually feel safer under Israeli control, this despite instances of unfair treatment because they are Arabs, and thus regarded with suspicion as a threat to the Jewish state. Yet very many Arab Christians refuse to make political capital out of the situation, unlike some of their leaders, and instead choose to turn the other cheek. That they have managed to obey this particularly challenging aspect of Scripture, a Christian virtue which sets us apart from other faiths, is humbling indeed. It also makes me ask: if they are able to do this, why do some supercessionist pro-Palestinian Christians insist on over-simplifying the conflict, exploiting the plight of these Arab Christians to make anti-Israeli political capital, which really only serves to increase the suspicion with which they are viewed by the Israeli state and population? Some Israelis I spoke with assumed, on the basis of the anti-Israel rhetoric they had heard from some Christians, that *all* Arab Christians were indeed enemies of Israel. I believe several pro-Palestinian Christians have sincere motives, but in many cases I see people with an irrational, pathological hatred of Israel, who exploit the difficulties of Arab Christians to promote their own theological and political agendas.

It is also disingenuous to blame all Arab Christian problems upon the Israelis. Ignoring the Islamist threat or a general suspicion held by many (though not all) Muslims towards Christians they regards as Crusaders is not only unhelpful, it is profoundly dishonest. This is an issue we should be praying earnestly about, lifting our fellow Arab Christians before God and seeking His care and protection for them. But if we simply choose to echo the Palestinian nationalist myth that *any* claim of Islamist persecution of Christians is a lie peddled by Israel for its own propaganda purposes, we are being less than honest in our prayer life.

By the same token, I would ask many Christian Zionists why they are not more vocal, as friends of Israel, in speaking out against the hounding of the tiny Messianic community in that land, or challenging the Israeli authorities to do more to protect them. Moreover, Israel's security policies have at times impacted unnecessarily upon Arab Christians. That is not to say Israel does not have a right to defend itself in difficult circumstances. I struggle with the hypocrisy of a world that exacts a higher standard from Israel than other countries. I have spent considerable time in Israel and seen first-hand the very real security threats and difficulties the country faces on a day to day basis. But neither should this mean we cannot criticise where Israel has done wrong. If Christian Zionists, the support of which Israel values greatly, were to stand up and challenge her over some of the problems Arab and Messianic Christians face, Israel would be far more likely to listen.

Neither does engaging with Israel on these issues somehow mean Christian Zionists are betraying their love for the Jewish people or their support for Israel. Criticism of some internal Israeli policies does not mean denying one's support for Israel or failing to recognise she faces real challenges and difficulties from external enemies seeking her annihilation. Thus, it is important for pro-Palestinian Christians to bear in mind the bigger picture, but by the same token Christian Zionists should take into account local issues and the internal situation. Yet many pro-Israel Christians feel – irrationally – that if they are critical of Israel *in any way* they are somehow denying the notion of the Jews as God's chosen people and are edging over into theological supercessionism. Of course not. Meanwhile I, as a good friend of Israel, nonetheless reject an 'Israel right or wrong' position. After all, if biblical Israel sinned, how can we say the secular nation of Israel today is without sin? Consider, for example, the view of one Arab Israeli pastor who leads a Messianic congregation and still sees the Jews as God's people. He asks how pro-Israel Christians can fight the sin of abortion in their own land yet ignore how in Israel thousands of abortions are carried out each year. Israel is not inerrant. Clearly, the more extreme Christian Zionists who ignore such facts are arguably guilty of idolatry (or 'Israelolatry', in this case).

An 'Israel right or wrong' position can also distort how we view our fellow Christians in the Holy Land. For example, one Christian shopkeeper in Jerusalem explained how one American Christian tourist couple came to his shop, asking if he was Jewish. He said he was an Arab but also a Christian, whereupon they left his shop, saying they wanted to buy from a Jewish shop in order to bless God's people. Such insensitivity by some Western Christians only serves to alienate Arab Christians.

If Christian Zionists are to avoid an 'Israel right or wrong' mentality, by the same token, Christian Palestinianism should reject an 'Israel is *always* wrong' position. The evidence on the ground suggests this is simply not true. I would much prefer to be a Christian in Israel, despite the problems they face there, than in many Muslim countries.

A Christian approach to this issue requires honesty, considerable nuance and reflection. I sincerely hope that as we continue to look at and comment upon this issue, we always strive to strip away all polemic and human instinct for simplistic or sensational pronouncements, in order to reach theologically-sound, sensitive and honest conclusions about the very difficult situation faced by Christians living in the Holy Land.

CHAPTER 8

Is the Gospel Relevant to
the Jewish People?
Tony Pearce

For I am not ashamed of the gospel, for it is the power of God for salvation to everyone who believes, to the Jew first and also to the Greek. For in it the righteousness of God is revealed from faith for faith, as it is written, "The righteous shall live by faith." (Rom 1:16-17)

In Romans 9-11 Paul deals with the issues relating to this question. In 9:4-5 he reminds us of what Israel has from the past: 'They are Israelites, and to them belong the adoption, the glory, the covenants, the giving of the law, the worship, and the promises. To them belong the patriarchs, and from their race, according to the flesh, is the Christ who is God over all, blessed forever.'

In chapter 10:1-4 he speaks of God's present will for Israel: 'Brothers, my heart's desire and prayer to God for them is that they may be saved. For I bear them witness that they have a zeal for God, but not according to knowledge. For, being ignorant of the righteousness of God, and seeking to establish their own, they did not submit to God's righteousness. For Christ is the end of the law for righteousness to everyone who believes.' It is clear Paul understood that salvation comes to Israel through the Gospel and that the means of them coming to this faith was to be the preaching of the Gospel: 'And how are they to believe in him of whom they have never heard? And how are they to hear without someone preaching? And how are they to preach unless they are sent? ...so faith comes from hearing, and hearing through the word of Christ' (Rom 10:14-15, 17).

In 11:25-27 he sees the future for Israel: 'Lest you be wise in your own sight, I want you to understand this mystery, brothers: a partial hardening has come upon Israel, until the fullness of the Gentiles has come in. And in this way all Israel will be saved, as it is written, "The Deliverer will come from Zion, he will banish ungodliness from Jacob; and this will be my covenant with them when I take away their sins."' The quotation is a composite quote from both Isaiah 59:20-21 and Jeremiah 31:31-34. For this future hope for Israel to be fulfilled, it is necessary for her to remain a people, with a covenant relationship with God, until the end of days and the return of the Messiah Jesus.

Some have commented on the fact that the future for Israel as given by Paul makes no mention of the land: 'The prophecy of Romans 11 is a prophecy that many Jews will return to Christ, but the land is not mentioned, nor is Israel mentioned as a political entity.'[1] When Paul wrote Romans the Jewish people were still in the land of Israel (under Roman occupation, admittedly), so a specific promise of a return to the land would have been out of place. It is difficult to imagine that the Apostle Paul could have conceived of the 'covenants' of which he wrote in this section of Romans without relating this to Genesis 15 and 17, in which God's covenant with Abraham and his descendants clearly relates to the land.

Putting these three chapters together it is clear Paul saw a continuation of the Jewish people after the birth of the church and sought their inclusion into the believing church. In fact he said it was the Gentiles who are included into the covenant God made with Israel, symbolised by the olive tree of Romans 11:11-24. For Romans 11:25-36 to be fulfilled it is necessary for Israel to remain a people until the return of the Messiah.

It is a remarkable testimony to the faithfulness of God's word that despite the dispersion of the Jewish people to the ends of the earth, persecution and assimilation, the Jews remain an

---

[1] J. Stott, 'Foreword,' in P. Johnstone and P Walker, eds. *The Promised Land* (Downers Grove, ILL: InterVarsity Press, 2000), 11.

identifiable people to this day. Even more remarkable that after the worst period of persecution they have ever known, the Nazi holocaust, 'am Israel chai' ('the people of Israel live') and are once again in the land promised to Abraham. And despite all the traumas of their history many Jewish people in the land of Israel and in the dispersion are coming to believe that Jesus, or Yeshua, to give Him His Hebrew name, is the Messiah.

One advantage the Apostle Paul had over us when he told Jewish people about the Messiah was he did not have nearly two thousand years of history to deal with. These years have caused an enormous barrier to be erected which prevents many Jewish people from even considering Jesus could be the Messiah. The barrier is actually two-fold – from the professing church and from the synagogue.

BARRIERS FROM WITHIN THE CHURCH

In Romans 10 Paul told Christians to pray for Israel that they might be saved. If we pray for our neighbour to be saved but he does not get saved, how do we respond to them? Do we go over to his house and throw stones through his window to show what a rotten person he is for not accepting the Lord? Of course not. We will try to show concern for him and to 'provoke him to jealousy' that he might want what we have (Romans 11:14). Sadly, the professing church has done much more than throw stones through the windows of the Jewish people. As the church rejected Paul's teaching not to cut themselves off from the Jewish roots of the faith, so it became anti-Semitic, and in the process actually denied much of the teaching of the Lord Jesus and the Apostles. John Chrystostom, considered a saint and church father who lived in the fourth century, wrote:

The Jews are the most worthless of all men. They are lecherous, greedy and rapacious. They are perfidious murderers of Christ. The Jews are the odious assassins of Christ and for killing God there is no expiation possible, no

> *indulgence or pardon. Christians may never cease vengeance and the Jews must live in servitude forever. God always hated the Jews. It is incumbent upon Christians to hate Jews.*[2]

When Constantine established Christianity as the official religion of the Roman Empire in 312, he issued many anti-Jewish laws. Jews were forbidden to accept converts, while every enticement was used to make them forsake Judaism. At the Council of Nicea in 325 he said, 'It is right to demand what our reason approves and that we should have nothing in common with the Jews.'[3]

Augustine taught that the Church had replaced Israel: 'For if we hold with a firm heart the grace of God which hath been given us, we are Israel, the seed of Abraham.'[4] He made what must be one of the most wrong-headed interpretations of Scripture ever, concerning Psalm 59.11: 'Kill them not, lest my people forget; make them totter by your power and bring them down.' This he interpreted to mean the vagabond Jews was a testimony of God's dealing with them in judgment according to the Scripture.[5]

In 1215 Pope Innocent III took up this theme when he condemned the Jews to eternal slavery by decreeing, 'The Jews against whom the blood of Jesus Christ calls out, although they ought not to be killed, lest the Christian people forget the Divine Law, yet as wanderers ought they remain upon the earth until their countenance be filled with shame.'[6]

Martin Luther, the founder of the German Reformation, hoped initially he would attract Jews to his Protestant faith, understanding they could not accept the superstitions and

---

[2] 'Homilae Adversus Iudaeos'.   John Chrysostom (c307-407) was a preacher with great powers of oratory from Antioch.
[3] In a letter to those not present at the Council (see Eusebius, Vita Const., Lib. iii., 18-20.), Fordham University's *Internet History Sourcebooks Project,* www.fordham.edu/halsall/source/const1-easter.html (accessed 18 February 2008).
[4] Augustine, *Expositions on the Book of Psalms* (vol 5), 114.3.
[5] Augustine, *The City of God,* 18.46.
[6] Innocent III, *Letter to the Count of Nevers,* 1208.

persecutions of Rome. But when they rejected his attempts to convert them, he turned on them and uttered words of hatred cited *verbatim* by the Nazis in their propaganda. He told the German princes how to deal with the Jews. This included setting their synagogues on fire, destroying their homes, forbidding rabbis to teach and depriving them of their prayer books. He said they should be forbidden to travel and to practice usury (the main occupation of Jews in the Middle Ages due to the restrictive laws of the time). In short he recommended enslaving them.[7]

Jewish people today are much more likely to know about this history than most Christians. For many, it is still played out in their experience of life. The singer Helen Shapiro gives her testimony of growing up in London in the 1950s and the shock of a child in primary school screaming at her, 'You killed Jesus.' Sometimes Christians say to me, 'Why can't Jewish people see that Jesus is the Messiah?' When we look at the image of Jesus that has been given to Jewish people through the centuries it is more remarkable that Jewish people like Helen Shapiro can see that Jesus is the Messiah.

In John's Gospel Jesus makes it clear who is responsible for his death:

> *For this reason the Father loves me, because I lay down my life that I may take it up again. No one takes it from me, but I lay it down of my own accord. I have authority to lay it down, and I have authority to take it up again. This charge I have received from my Father.* (John 10:17-18)

The implication of this is clear. Jesus Himself takes responsibility for His own death. It happens at the time and manner of His choosing, in order that He might fulfil the Father's will by dying

---

[7] Martin Luther, *Concerning the Jews and Their Lies* (1543 tract). For further details of Luther's view of the Jews see M. Vlach, 'Martin Luther and Supersessionism',
www.theologicalstudies.org/luther_supersessionism.html (last accessed 18 February 2009).

as the sacrifice for the sins of the world and rising again from the dead to give eternal life to those who receive Him. No human being, Jew or Gentile, has the right or the power to take Jesus' life from Him against His will.

This fulfils the prophecy of Isaiah 53, which states concerning the sufferings of the Messiah, `Yet it was the will of the Lord to crush him; he has put him to grief' (Isa 53:10). In this prophecy the responsibility for Messiah's sufferings is placed on God Himself. 'It was the will of the Lord to crush him' means Jesus was put to death to fulfil the will of God.

According to the Book of Hebrews, those who believe come to 'Jesus, the mediator of a new covenant, and to the sprinkled blood that speaks a better word than the blood of Abel' (Heb 12:24). The blood of Abel spoke of vengeance for Cain's sin of murder (Genesis 4), but the blood of Jesus speaks of mercy and forgiveness. Wrong church teaching however has turned this on its head and used the verse in Matthew's Gospel, 'His blood be upon us and on our children' (Matt 27:25), to claim that the suffering of the Jewish people is the result of a self-inflicted curse, and even that Christians are therefore justified in persecuting the Jewish people in Jesus' name.

Nothing could be further from the truth. Jesus Himself prayed from the cross, 'Father, forgive them, for they know not what they do,' (Luke 23:34), thus expressing God's will that even those responsible for the death of Jesus, whether Jewish or Gentile, should find forgiveness through His name. Do we base our theology on the words of an enraged crowd or on the words of the Lord Jesus?

The answer to Jesus' prayer was to be found not long afterwards in the preaching of the Apostles. When Peter preached in the Temple after the Day of Pentecost, before him were people who had really been responsible for the death of Jesus in that they called for Him to be crucified. But even to them there was a message of hope and forgiveness. Explaining the meaning of the death and resurrection of Jesus Peter said, 'And now, brothers, I know that you acted in ignorance, as did also your rulers. But what God foretold by the mouth of all the prophets, that his Christ would suffer, he thus fulfilled. Repent therefore, and turn again, that your sins may be blotted out (Acts 3:17-19).

The statement which really tells us who was responsible for the death of Jesus is to be found in Acts 4.27-28: 'For truly in this city there were gathered together against your holy servant Jesus, whom you anointed, both Herod and Pontius Pilate, along with the Gentiles and the peoples of Israel, to do whatever your hand and your plan had predestined to take place.'

In this prayer all categories of people are implicated: Herod and Pontius Pilate with the Gentiles and the people of Israel. The Gentiles are actually mentioned before the people of Israel, therefore they have no right to claim any superiority or judgmental attitude towards the Jews. It is clear the physical act of crucifying Jesus was carried out on the orders of the Roman governor, by Roman soldiers in the Roman way. Strangely no one has ever suggested the Italians killed Jesus and should be placed under a curse because of this! All this happened 'to do whatever your hand and your plan had predestined to take place', in other words to fulfil the predetermined plan of God. So again the ultimate responsibility for the death of Jesus rests with God Himself in order to fulfil His purposes.

A number of Christians react to anti-Semitism within Christianity by taking the view that Christians should not share the Gospel with Jewish people. Some then become involved in pro-Israel activities or in dialogue with Jewish people and deny Jews need salvation through Jesus the Messiah. A noted example of this view is John Hagee, who organises events to honour Israel and raises large sums of money from Evangelical Christians to give to Jewish charities in Israel. Hagee has said,

The Jewish people have a relationship to God through the law of God as given through Moses. I believe that every Gentile person can only come to God through the cross of

Christ. I believe that every Jewish person who lives in the light of the Torah, which is the word of God, has a relationship with God and will come to redemption. The law of Moses is sufficient enough to bring a person into the knowledge of God until God gives him a greater revelation. And God has not.[8]

But the whole message of the New Testament is that God has given a greater revelation in Jesus. The book of Hebrews explains this 'better covenant' which we enter into through faith in the Messiah. In fact, if Jesus is not the Messiah of the Jewish people then He is not the Messiah of anyone, because our very concept of Messiah comes from the Jews.

BARRIERS FROM WITHIN THE SYNAGOGUE

Modern Judaism fits in with Paul's words in Romans 10 where he speaks of Jewish people 'seeking to establish their own righteousness' but not submitting to the 'righteousness of God. For Christ / Messiah is the end of the law for righteousness to everyone who believes.' Paul is saying Jesus the Messiah provides the solution to the sin problem and if we miss this then we are going to end up trying to establish our own system of religious good works in order to find salvation.

It can be shown that all religious systems including nominal Christianity do exactly this. All religions basically offer some system of good works in order to cancel out our sins and gain credit with God.   Because none of them are based on God's revelation they all fail. In modern Judaism it can be shown there is a religious system which is based on their own Messiah, their own way of atoning for sins and their own holy books.

---

[8] 'San Antonio fundamentalist battles anti-Semitism', *Houston Chronicle*, April 30, 1988.

Their Own Messiah

One of the most common objections to Jesus being the Messiah coming from Jewish people is that there has been no peace since Jesus came, and therefore He cannot be the Messiah. This is based on the view that the Messiah must fulfil Scriptures such as Isaiah 2:1-4 and 11-12 when He comes. Isaiah 2 is accepted as being a Messianic passage by the synagogue and the church. It promises a time when 'nation shall not lift up sword against nation, neither shall they learn war anymore.' Another objection is the Christian view of Jesus as the Son of God, and the implication that God is a plural unity of Father, Son and Holy Spirit.

According to Maimonides (1135-1204), the pre-eminent Jewish rabbi and teacher of the Middle Ages, the Messiah has to complete the following three tasks:

1. Re-gather the dispersed Jewish people to Israel
2. Rebuild the Temple in Jerusalem
3. Make world peace.[9]

By contrast it is pointed out since the coming of Jesus the following has happened:

1. The Jewish people were dispersed into the nations
2. The Temple in Jerusalem was destroyed
3. There have been wars and persecutions ever since

Of course, Jesus never claimed He would bring world peace following His first coming and prophesied a long period of 'wars and rumours of wars' (Matt 24:6), the destruction of the Temple (Luke 19:41-44) and the dispersion of the Jewish people into the nations (Luke 21:20-24). There will be a reversal of this process at the end of days when Jerusalem will no longer be 'trampled underfoot by the Gentiles' (Luke 21:24), and its people will welcome Jesus as returning Messiah with the Messianic greeting 'Blessed is he who comes in the name of the Lord' (Matt 23:39).

---

[9] Maimonides Hilchos Melachim 11.1 and 4 from the Mishneh Torah.

There is a hope for the time of peace and justice, of which the Prophets spoke, being fulfilled after the return of the Lord Jesus in the Millennium (Revelation 20), or Messianic Age. Of course, the problem of explaining this to Jewish people today is much of the church takes the amillennial view that these prophecies are fulfilled in the church reigning today or in heaven. In fact much of the church misses the point about the future reign of the Messiah after His return, just as the Jewish people miss the fact that He has already come as Suffering Servant.

Isaiah actually gives two different portraits of the Messiah, one as a reigning king (Isaiah 2) and the other as a suffering servant (Isaiah 53). Isaiah 53:3, 5-6 describes the servant of the Lord as one who is 'despised and rejected by men; a man of sorrows, and acquainted with grief… he was wounded for our transgressions; he was crushed for our iniquities; upon him was the chastisement that brought us peace, and with his stripes we are healed. All we like sheep have gone astray; we have turned— every one—to his own way; and the Lord has laid on him the iniquity of us all.' Modern Judaism tries to interpret this passage as applying to the sufferings of Israel as taught by the French rabbi Rashi (1040-1105). However, according to Arnold Fruchtenbaum, 'Every rabbi prior to Rashi, without exception, viewed Isaiah 53 as describing Messiah. When Rashi first proposed that this passage spoke of the nation of Israel, he sparked a fierce debate with his contemporaries. Maimonides stated very clearly that Rashi is completely wrong and going against the traditional Jewish viewpoint.'[10]

There are various reasons why Isaiah 53 cannot refer to the sufferings of Israel on behalf of the Gentiles. The Suffering Servant of Isaiah 53 bears the sins of others. If the servant is Israel then Isaiah must be a Gentile because the people he identifies with ('all we like sheep') have their iniquity laid on him (Israel?). Of course, this is impossible and Isaiah is identifying the sins of

---

[10] Arnold Fruchtenbaum, *Messianic Christology* (San Antonio, TX: Ariel, 1998), 54.

himself and his people Israel being laid on this servant of the Lord. Isaiah has spent much of his prophecy speaking of the sins of Israel, as we see in the first chapter of his book: 'Israel does not know, my people do not understand. Ah, sinful nation, a people laden with iniquity' (Isa 1:3-4). A sinful people cannot bear the sins of others. Only one who is without sin Himself, as Paul states in 2 Corinthians 5:21, 'For our sake he made him to be sin who knew no sin, so that in him we might become the righteousness of God.'

Isaiah 53 was perfectly fulfilled by the sacrificial death of the Lord Jesus as recorded in the New Testament. The New Testament clearly teaches that the same Jesus will come again, this time as King of Kings and Lord of Lords and that He will judge the world in righteousness (Matt 24, Mark 13, Luke 21, Acts 1, Rev 6-19). In the time between His first and second coming the Gospel will go out to all nations to bring in the harvest of souls who are saved through repentance and faith in the Lord Jesus as Saviour / Messiah.

While the Messianic prophecies do not specifically state there will be two comings of the same Messiah, it is clear that there are two different portraits of the Messiah, one as a Suffering Servant and one as a Reigning King. There are rabbinic writings which acknowledge this and try to explain it by saying there are two Messiahs, one known as Messiah son of Joseph, who suffers and is then exalted as Joseph was in Genesis, and the other known as Messiah son of David who reigns as a king like David.[11] The better explanation is there is one Messiah who comes on two different occasions and whose name is Jesus / Yeshua.

On the issue of the divinity of the Messiah there are a number of prophecies which do indicate the coming one will be more than just a great man who brings peace. In Isaiah 9:6 we read of one to be born as a child, but who will also be Mighty God, Everlasting Father. In Micah 5.2 the one to be born in Bethlehem will have

---

[11] For details on this see David Baron, *Visions and Prophecies of Zechariah* (Whitefish, MT: Kessinger, 2007), 441.

His origins in the 'days of eternity'. Only God has his origins in eternity. In Zechariah 14:4 the one whose feet stand on the Mount of Olives at the end of days is identified as the LORD (Yahweh). In Judaism, this prophecy is believed to be about the Messiah and it ties in with the New Testament promise of the return of Jesus (Acts 1:11-12).

There are also passages which speak of God as a plural unity in the Torah. In the very first verse of the Bible we read, 'In the beginning God created the heavens and the earth' (Gen 1:1). The word for "God" (Elohim) is a masculine plural noun. The word for "created" (bara) is a singular verb. The very first sentence in the Bible, with a plural noun and a singular verb, opens up the possibility of God being a plural unity. In Genesis 1:26 God said, 'Let us make man in our image, after our likeness.' Why not 'Let me make man in my image'? It cannot be that God is speaking to the angels, because man is not made in the image of angels. The rabbinic explanation, that it is the plural of majesty, does not add up either since there is no example in the Bible of kings addressing themselves in the plural. The likely explanation for this and other occasions where God speaks in the plural of Himself (Gen 11:7, Isa 6.8) is that God is a plural unity.

Atonement
Modern Judaism does not deal with the sin problem in the way the Torah requires. In order to cover sin and escape from its penalty (death) there must be repentance and sacrifice of another who dies in our place. Under the covenant with Moses this was the animal which sacrificed its blood (and therefore died) in accordance with the commandments given in the Torah. This was the only way in which the barrier between God and humanity, caused by sin, could be removed. God is holy and we are not, and the only way we can relate to the Holy One is on His terms, not ours. The Lord makes it clear He requires the shedding of blood in order to be able to come into relationship with his people. In Leviticus 17.11 we read: 'For the life of the flesh is in the blood, and I have given it for you on

the altar to make atonement for your souls, for it is the blood that makes atonement by the life.'

However, modern Judaism teaches that the blood of atonement is no longer required today. When the Temple was destroyed in 70 CE by the Romans, the Sanhedrin reconvened in Yavneh under the leadership of Rabbi Yochanan ben Zakkai, who developed a theology based on some verses of the Bible which seem to point to sacrifices being unnecessary as a means of mediating between God and humanity. For example, 'What to me is the multitude of your sacrifices? says the Lord; I have had enough of burnt offerings of rams and the fat of well-fed beasts; I do not delight in the blood of bulls, or of lambs, or of goats... bring no more vain offerings; incense is an abomination to me' (Isa 1:11, 13).

Based on these Scriptures Judaism developed a theology which relegated the sacrificial system to ancient history. The fact that the Temple no longer stood and therefore there was no access to the place appointed by God to offer the sacrifices seemed to confirm this view. Therefore the Rabbis decreed that God was able to forgive sins through repentance, prayers, fasting and good deeds which replaced the blood of the animal sacrifices.

So does God say that sacrifices are not needed to cover sins? In Isaiah 1 God tells His people they are offering sacrifices without sincerity and continuing in sin at the same time. God is not actually saying, 'You don't need to offer any sacrifices.' What He is saying is 'Your sacrifices are meaningless because you are just going through the outward motions of pleasing me while your hearts and your actions are far from me.' He is calling on them to repent *and* to offer the sacrifices from a true heart, not to repent *instead* of offering the sacrifices.

Under the old covenant the worshipper found forgiveness through repentance and faith in the sin offering prescribed by the Torah. He recognised he deserved to die, but God in His mercy accepted this sacrifice in his place. The blood of the animal itself only had value in that it pointed forward to the blood of the

Messiah who was yet to come. Under the New Covenant the same principle applies. We find forgiveness through repentance and faith in the blood of the Messiah shed for our sins:

> *(Christ) has appeared once for all at the end of the ages to put away sin by the sacrifice of himself. 27 And just as it is appointed for man to die once, and after that comes judgment, 28 so Christ, having been offered once to bear the sins of many, will appear a second time, not to deal with sin but to save those who are eagerly waiting for him.* (Heb 9:26-28).

Under the New Covenant the same principle operates as under the Old Covenant: that those who come to God must repent of their sins and put their trust in the sacrifice He has appointed. Under the Old Covenant it was the blood of the sacrificed animal. Under the New Covenant it is the much better sacrifice of the blood of Jesus the Messiah. Through accepting this sacrifice we find our way back to a covenant relationship with God.

Holy books
In a way both Judaism and Christianity acknowledge that the Old Testament / Tenach on its own is not enough. Christians believe we need the New Testament to reveal the real meaning of Old Testament events. Judaism rejects the New Testament and therefore does not like to refer to the Hebrew Bible as the 'Old' Testament. However Judaism has its own additional book, or rather a great library of books, known as the Talmud.

It is believed that when God gave the written word to Israel He also gave the Oral Torah, which was not written down but passed on by word of mouth from generation to generation, eventually to be codified in the Rabbinic writings known as the Mishna and the Gemara compiled in the Palestinian Talmud around 400 CE and the Babylonian Talmud around 500 CE. Rabbi Simmons writes:

The Oral Torah is not an interpretation of the Written Torah. In fact, the Oral Torah preceded the Written Torah. When the Jewish people stood at Mount Sinai 3,300 years ago, God communicated the 613 commandments, along with a detailed, practical explanation of how to fulfil them. At that point in time, the teachings were entirely oral. It wasn't until 40 years later, just prior to Moses' death and the Jewish people entering the Land of Israel, that Moses wrote the scroll of the written Torah (known as the Five Books of Moses) and gave it to the Jewish people.[12]

Admittedly we do not have any detailed record of how the Torah came to be written down, but at the same time we have no mention in the Bible of the existence of an oral Torah separate from the written Torah. Here is something very strange. If God had given Moses both the written and the oral Torah surely something would have been mentioned in the written Torah pointing to the existence of this other teaching, which was necessary to understand the written Torah. But what do we find? Not a word about it.

In fact we find evidence to the contrary. It is hard to see how Rabbi Simmons can justify the statement that the oral Torah preceded the written Torah when Exodus 24 says 'Moses *wrote down all the words of the Lord*... then he took the *Book of the Covenant* and *read* it in the hearing of the people' (Ex 24:4-7. According to the text this happened immediately after Moses came down from the Mountain.

Moreover the Book of Joshua tells us Joshua (to whom Moses is supposed to have communicated the unwritten oral Torah) possessed a written word, which he read to the people of Israel as they entered the Land. This written word contained *all* that Moses had passed down:

---

[12] 'What is Oral Torah?' Aish ha Torah's Discovery Seminar, Aish website:
www.aish.com/shavuotsinai/shavuotsinaidefault/what_is_the_oral_torah$.asp (last accessed 19 February 2009).

And afterward he (Joshua) read all the words of the law, *the blessing and the curse, according to all that is* written in the Book of the Law. *There was not a word of all that Moses commanded that Joshua did not* read *before all the assembly of Israel, and the women, and the little ones, and the sojourners who lived among them.* (Josh 8:34-35)

It is hard to reconcile these verses with the idea of an unwritten oral Torah, which precedes the written Torah and is equally inspired given by God at Mount Sinai.

In practice the Talmud is generally treated as more important than the Bible in the life of Jewish people. I once attended a lecture at a Jewish outreach centre in London during which the rabbi spoke about the Oral Torah. He told the following story found in the talmudic tractate *Bava Mezia* 59b. This follows a discussion according to halakha (halakha means the body of Jewish law supplementing the scriptural law and forming the legal part of the Talmud) in which the rabbis debated whether an oven that had become impure could be purified. While almost all the sages felt it could not be, Rabbi Eliezer, a lone voice but a great scholar, disagreed:

> *On that day, Rabbi Eliezer put forward all the arguments in the world, but the Sages did not accept them. Finally, he said to them, 'If the halakha is according to me, let that carob tree prove it.' He pointed to a nearby carob tree, which then moved from its place a hundred cubits, and some say, four hundred cubits. They said to him 'One cannot bring a proof from the moving of a carob tree.'*
>
> *Said Rabbi Eliezer, 'If the halakha is according to me, may that stream of water prove it.' The stream of water then turned and flowed in the opposite direction. They said to him, 'One cannot bring a proof from the behavior of a stream of water.'*
>
> *Said Rabbi Eliezer, 'If the halakha is according to me, may the walls of the House of Study prove it.' The walls of the*

House of Study began to bend inward. Rabbi Joshua then rose up and rebuked the walls of the House of Study, 'If the students of the Wise argue with one another in halakha," he said, 'what right have you to interfere?' In honor of Rabbi Joshua, the walls ceased to bend inward; but in honor of Rabbi Eliezer, they did not straighten up, and they remain bent to this day.

Then said Rabbi Eliezer to the Sages, 'If the halakha is according to me, may a proof come from Heaven.' Then a heavenly voice went forth and said, 'What have you to do with Rabbi Eliezer? The halakha is according to him in every place.' Then Rabbi Joshua rose up on his feet, and said, 'It is not in the heavens' (Deuteronomy 30:12).

What did he mean by quoting this? Said Rabbi Jeremiah, 'He meant that since the Torah has been given already on Mount Sinai, we do not pay attention to a heavenly voice, for You have written in Your Torah, 'Decide according to the majority' (Exodus 23:2).

Rabbi Nathan met the prophet Elijah. He asked him, 'What was the Holy One, Blessed be He, doing in that hour?' Said Elijah, 'He was laughing and saying, 'My children have defeated me, my children have defeated me.'

The British-Jewish scholar and writer Hyam Maccoby has commented: 'This extraordinary story strikes the keynote of the Talmud. God is a good father who wants His children to grow up and achieve independence. He has given them His Torah, but now wants them to develop it....' [13]

Hyam Maccoby actually misses the real point of this story. It means the Sages of Israel are treated as being a higher authority than God Himself and that the words of the Oral Torah are greater

---

[13] Source: Joseph Telushkin, *Jewish Literacy: The Most Important Things to Know About the Jewish Religion, Its People and Its History* (NY: William Morrow, 1991). Available on the Jewish Virtual Library: www.jewishvirtuallibrary.org/jsource/Judaism/Halakha_&_aggadata_&_midrash.html (last accessed 4 March 2009).

in importance than the words of God in the Bible. This was the issue Jesus faced with the religious leaders of His day, likewise Christianity today when writings of men and traditions become of greater importance than the word of God.

The Torah shows us that we all fall short of the glory of God and need to be made right with God by repentance and faith in the sacrifice God has appointed. Under the old covenant this was through the blood of the animals offered on Yom Kippur. Under the new covenant it is through the blood of the Messiah. In this way Messiah Jesus becomes our bridge to God, fulfilling His word, 'I am the way, and the truth, and the life. No one comes to the Father except through me' (John 14:6).

Yeshua, Jesus, is the Messiah of whom Moses and the Prophets spoke, who has mediated the new covenant through which we can find the true bridge to God. Through His death and resurrection He has paid the price required for sin and made it possible for all humanity, Jewish and Gentile, to come to know God's forgiveness and eternal life. Those who truly accept Him as Messiah, Saviour and Lord experience the new birth which Jesus spoke about to Nicodemus which empowers us by the Holy Spirit to walk in newness of life and gives us the desire to keep His commandments. Although we remain liable to sin and still fall short of the glory of God, the blood Jesus shed is sufficient to cover our sins and to give us peace with God so that we know that when we appear before God on the Day of Judgment He will receive us into eternal life in His kingdom which shall never pass away.

More details on the subject explored in this chapter can be found in Tony Pearce's book The Messiah Factor *available from Tony Pearce, Box BM 4226, London, WC1N 3XX.*

Scripture Index

Genesis

1:1	55-6, 88, 150
1:26	150
3	88
4	144
11:7	150
12:1ff	64, 66, 69, 71
15:6	72
15:13-21	66, 69, 71, 140
15:18	76-80
17:7-8	111, 140
22:18	79

Exodus

4:22	1
12:19, 45	29n
12:48-49	29n
19:6	27, 67n
20:10	29n
23:2	155
24:4-7	153

Leviticus

14:22	28
16:29	29n
17:11	151-52
17:12, 15	29n
18:26	29n
18:28	75
19:36	43

23:22	28n
24:16	29n
25:23	74

Numbers

9:14	29n
15:14-16	28
15:30	30
16:34	23
19:10	29n
35:15	28n

Deuteronomy

4:34	27
5:1	29n
9:4-5, 24-29	75
10:18-19	28, 28n
14:29	28n
24:17, 19-21	28n
26:11	29n
26:13	28n
27:19	28n
28:64-67	89-90
30:3-5	90
30:12	155
31:12	29n

Joshua

7:25	23
8:34-35	154

Judges		78:54	75
		83:3-4	45-46
16:21-30	41, 122	105:8-11	111
		122:6	45
Ruth			
		Proverbs	
1:16	29		
		11:22	54
2 Samuel		25:11	54
		29:20	42
7	69		
7:23	27	**Isaiah**	
16:22	23		
		1:3-4	149
1 Kings		1:11, 13	151
		2	147, 148
11:36	78	5:7	66n
		6:8	150
2 Kings		7:14	39
		9:6-7	104, 149
5:1-14	72	41:8-9	1
		42:6f	72
1 Chronicles		43	89
		44:1-3	1, 37
21:15-28	39	44:21	1
		49	89
2 Chronicles		49:3	1
		52:8	75
13:22	51	53	144, 148-49
		53:10	144
Ezra		59:20-21	35, 36, 140
		61:6	67n
9:2	31	65:17	67n
Psalms		**Jeremiah**	
2	69	7:6	28n
2:6-7	104	30 - 33	89
59:11	142	30:7	112

30:10	1
31:31-38	35, 37n, 66, 70, 90-91, 92-93, 140
46:27	1

Ezekiel

18:31	37
22:7	28n
36 – 39	89
36:26-27	37
37:1-14	75
47:23	29n

Daniel

12:1	112

Hosea

11:1	1, 39, 57-58

Joel

1:15	121
2:1ff	37-38, 75, 121
3:14	121

Amos

8:5	43

Obadiah

15	121
19	121

Micah

4:1-4	38
4 - 5	69
5:2	149-50
6:11	43

Habakkuk

2:4	72

Zechariah

2:8	103
2:14	75
8:1-3	97
8:23	1, 37n
9:9	104
12:1ff	37, 89
12:10	37, 38
13	89
13:1	37
14:4	150

Matthew

1:1	69
1:23	39
2:2	38n
2:15	39, 57
3:9	71
5:39	135-36
7:28	33
8:11	71
9:27	77n
10:5-6	33
12:39-41	62
13:47-50	36n
15:24	33

15:31	33	18:31ff	68
19:28	73	19:41-44	147
20:30-31	77n	20:9-19	66
21:9	77n	21	149
21:37-45	66, 66n	21:20-24	91, 147
21:45	55	21:24	38n, 147
22:41-46	77n	22:16-18	36n
23:37	33, 45n	23:2	31n
23:39	147	23:34	144
24 - 25	39n, 59-60, 92, 149	24:27	68
24:6	147		
24:16-20	39n	**John**	
24:21	111	1:1ff	55-56
24:24	58	1:45	68
24:29-31	39n	1:48	56
24:34-35	92	1:49	38n
25:1	36n	3:5	33, 56
25:6	118	3:18	80
27:11	38n	4:22	1, 71
27:25	144	8:56	71
		10:17-18	143
Mark		11:48	31n
		12:13	33, 38n
12:1-12	66, 66n	14:1-3	116
13	149	14:3	104
		14:6	80, 156
Luke			
		Acts	
1:31-33	77n		
1:68	33	1	149
2:25-39	104	1:6-7	34, 73, 76
2:25	33	1:7	73
2:32	33	1:11-12	150
7:5	31n	2:1ff	37
9:25	11	3:17-19	144-45
11:29-32	62	3:18	68
11:52	55	4:10	80
13:34	33, 45n	4:27-28	145

162

7:19	31	10:1-4	141
10:22	31n	10:2	xiv
13:23	35n	10:12	34n
15	72-73	10:14-15	139
16:3	72	10:17	139
17:2-5	70	10:19	34
17:26	74	11:1	34, 117
18:18	72	11:11-12	35, 79
24:2	32n	11:15	79
24:17	32n, 34	11:13-24	20, 29, 33-34,
26:4	32n, 34		79, 140, 141
28:19	32n	11:25-32	111
		11:25-26	8-24, 19, 22,

Romans

			35, 35n, 36-37,
			140
1:8	79	11:28-36	35
1:16	34, 139	11:28	96n, 103
1:20	79	11:29	xiii, 35
2 - 3	94	11:30-32	16
2:9	34	11:33	xiv
2:28-29	19		
3:3-4	91	*1 Corinthians*	
3:6	79		
3:19	79	10:18	11, 13n, 16
4:11-12	71	12:13	34n
4:13	67, 79		
4:16	69	*2 Corinthians*	
5:12-13	79		
8:19-22	118	5:21	149
9 - 11	6, 18-19, 34-		
	35, 73-74, 75,	*Galatians*	
	80, 120, 139,		
	141, 146	3:28	34n, 66-67, 70
9:1-5	15-16, 34,	3:29	71
	34n	4:26	78n
9:4-5	1, 17, 139	6:15	67
9:6, 7	11, 33n, 40	6:16	11-15, 33n, 63
9:7-13	18, 95		
9:16	96n		

Ephesians

1:14	75
2:11-14	29, 70
2:12-13	33, 67

Colossians

3:11	34n

1 Thess

1:10	111
2:14-16	66, 70
4:15-18	104, 116

2 Timothy

4:8	117

Hebrews

8:13	95n
9:26-28	152
10:1	77
11	77-79
12:22	78n
12:24	144

James

1:19-20	42

1 Peter

2:9	67, 94

2 Peter

3:12-13	67n

Jude

	60

Revelation

2:4	118
9:1ff	37
11:15	36n
12:10	36n
20	148
21:2	35n
21:9-26	78n
21:10	78
22:20	118